Selfless Letters:
Caring Desires, Scorned Egos

POET CRUCIAL &
ARTIE BRYANT

Publishing Service By: Pen Legacy® (www.penlegacy.com)

Typesetting By: Carla M. Dean

Cover Illustration By: Demitrius Bullock
(demitriusbullock@gmail.com, http://www.motionillustrationz.com)

Interior Illustration By: Demitrius Bullock, Darian Bryant & Lori Joy

Library of Congress Cataloging – in-Publication Data has been applied for.

Paperback ISBN: 978-1-7362575-4-8

PRINTED IN THE UNITED STATES OF AMERICA

Thank You for purchasing Our Book,
and Welcome to Our Book Project.

"Selfless Letters: Caring Desires, Scorned Egos"

Selfless Letters:
Caring Desires, Scorned Egos

Love & Pain

Times are crazier than ever,
Social Media got married folks claiming to be single,
Single folks claiming they want to be married,
A Bona Fide Racist in the White House
under the guise of Forty Five,
Enacting a modern day cultural purge,
Until all Melanated Black & Brown folks
eventually die,
Systematically sending
his Proud Boy Law Enforcement Thugs
to kneel on our necks,
While he stands in front of the media
with every other word of his being a lie,
As more Melanated Faces are openly lost
right in front of our eyes,
Blatantly No Fear
killing right in front of Us,
Leaving those who cared behind,
To Protest and Cry,
We are a Beautiful Race
of Melanated People
just trying to navigate this world we live in
of *"Love & Pain,"*
Constantly Fighting & Searching for Freedom
while always having loss and death thrown in Our Face,
Knowing Unconditionally…
That GOD would never forsake
Our Original Chocolate Complexion,
Though it's the main stream perception
so caught up in their Falsified Historical Misconception,
That innately from fear in their crushing insecurity
whether seen or unseen,

They portray and act out their growing internal agony
on GOD'S Melanated Us,
So their mistrust continues to grow,
All the while their damaged ego shows
because mistrust & betrayal
it's all they actually know,
And in this betrayal sadly
with its seeds and roots,
Now grow strong in the conscious
of Our Black & Brown Beautiful Culture,
And when Genuine Love is attacked,
Whether it be a Racist ...
Family ...
Friend ...
Foe ...
Or Lover ...
That becomes a very dangerous thing,
I've heard it once stated
it's a Thin Line Between Love & Hate,
As I believe the same is true for *"Love & Pain,"*
The heartbreak and regret feels exactly the same,
Just seeking the Caring & Warmth
of My Manifested Loving Queen
that would define forever loyalty,
A selfless security slowly being lost by some
in Our Culture,
Whether it's between
the Black/Brown Man & Black/Brown Woman
the Black/Brown Woman & Black/Brown Woman,
Or the Black/Brown Man & the Black/Brown Man
back to the Black/Brown Woman & the Black/Brown Man,
Too many of Us quietly living in agony
while feeling scorned daily in life,
Which then adds to our interactions
with one another being quite trife,
So then in some cases,
The Cultural Connection
is sadly rife with defeat,

We must therefore find the Patience Culturally
with one another,
Through Our past pain-filled tears
to find the admiration for each other,
Like a childbirth anew of Cultural Relationships,
A Re-Birth amongst Our People
of genuine desire from one to the other,
To in turn reflect the simple pleasure and pride that glows
in Our Melanin,
Consistently each day finally
From and To one another in the end.

Poet Crucial ©*2020*

Love & Pain

What if…
What if society cared less about your notoriety and attention
was paid more to your core?
What if I could Dream of a fairy tale world
with no strife?
My life would be the very first that I researched

In the words of 44
"It's time for Change "
To Hell with All Of That
I changed my mind, Locked in on me and mine
Locked in on passing this test of Covid times

Love is potent…
Love leaves me vulnerable and open…
Love is disguised and blind…
Love is so strange…
Love is a one of a kind Pain

Loving a nation that doesn't love me or my block
A nation that lacks empathy and compassion Its all haves
and have nots
The hatred is dearly defined in actions that used to be hidden
"I can't breathe"
What the hell is this box that we've been giving to live in?

We love to hate and hate to love…
What if everything was created equal?
What if we lived in a land of the free…
A land that was free for all races and all people?
What if this land was a home of the brave?
What if there never was a massa or a shackle…and
What if there were never ever any slaves?

I'm in love with this skin that I'm in and Loving yours too is
the GOAL
Hate hasn't tainted or painted my soul
I'm anchored strength through any pandemic
Cut from a cloth that looks for fires and
Stands straight in it
Keep your distance, 6 feet at least
2020 critics, overcrowded clinics
Standing on Faith and my love pillars
We ain't no quitters and we ain't no killers
But don't push me….

Love and Pain never reigns together
Enticed like fire and ice or day and night
FOR YOU ARE MY BROTHER!
After the storms
the sun sheds light on all struggles
Caring or Scorned
We can't have one without having the other

Artie Bryant

A Soul's Reflection

In My Soul,
From the beginning
when our paths first crossed,
As a Man I felt then,
What I still feel now
only to a deeper degree…
That your Karma's heat is intense
sustained by a Woman
tired of all the games
and Man's simple BS,
Asking for only …
One Righteous Brother
who could look you in the eyes
and read the deep novel of Your Soul,
Treat you in a way
that you wished to be treated
but without having to be told,
Touched in a way
that only Your Heart could feel,
and saying all the right things
without uttering a word,
And from Your Soul's Reflection
I knew I was the one.
Connected to Your Essence,
Ever so intently
wanting to drink you in,
To have us mesh,

And watch our spirits dance
as only My Soul could to Yours,
Your realness attracts many
even some from your past
with only the truth between us
fueling our vibe,
Maintaining our cosmic connection
which has our hearts beat as one,
It never mattered what others thought
including our family and friends,
As long as between us
it always stayed real,
So thru the events
that have just taken place
overcoming our trials and tribulations
it may shake our foundation,
Unless what we feel
remains true to one another,
Images that Reflect
true heated passion from the Soul,
We will always remain the same
You to Me,
And finally I always to You.

Poet Crucial ©2001

Addiction

I got a confession ...
That I have an addiction
caught up straight on the chase,
Ever since that first hit,
This monkey on my back
as I ride the chocolate white horse
grows intense every day,
It calls me at times
whispering my name ...
"Crucial,"
This jonz
I try to control
wakes me in the middle of the night
cold sweats and chills
from a deep deep sleep,
It's a hunger I feel within
no matter how many times
I feed this desire,
It fuels my want
for more every day,
A straight fiend is what I am,
To understand my case
is to know my habit
to define what it is I crave,
All women possess one
make no mistake about it,
But they are all just not the same,
Cause see mentally first

she has to be on point,
Physically able to keep my eye
in order to have the power
to spark my internal flame,
That begins my high,
Then what she has
6 inches below her belly button
builds my base
to make me feel so free,
Floating like a kite
oblivious to my surroundings
lost in a psychedelic orgasmic haze,
The trip this woman sends me on
starts my mind to wander,
Makes me think
nothing has ever felt this good,
Except for when I was a fetus
living in perfect balance
for 9 months inside my Mother's womb,
Where karmic relativity
was equaled with harmonious understanding,
This woman and I
mentally we are in sync
where intimately I'm smoked out
on just her brand of crack,
Raising my temperature
like Gator with Jungle Fever,
My friends saying to me
I remind them of that New Jack
from down in the city,
They just don't know,
And I'm not the one to tell
though from this woman's smile,

When I go downtown
no one,
Not even Pookie got a thing on me,
So with loving passion
and her approval,
I'm an abuser of her substance
enough I want her to be My Wife,
Spending the rest of my days
on her emotional high,
But since I'm an addict
I know it's important,
That I take her and us,
Just one day at a precious time.

Poet Crucial ©2003

Black Butterfly

You were born to sing, her voice is music to his ears
Ms Queen sing eloquently to your King
But her tongue gets devilish and lashing
Verbal lacerations smashing her King's world at the drop of
any dime

Belittle that man when you demanded Queen treatment
Adam's RIB turned Adam's little girl…
so much anger in a split second a lyrical weapon spitting like
AK's straight to his Face
"respect that Queen" is the two-way lane
Respect this KING and its two-way place

True Love is bliss with a bond tighter than a fist
true Love is evident when bystanders can't resist
stop and stare for a glance or glare
with hopeful aspirations for tips on the chance at romance

A Butterfly emerged from her cocoon
She makes any room stand still
for a goddess has walked from mythology with no apologies
on her beauty or her real
accept her for who she is
Black Butterfly

Artie Bryant

Tainted Mind

In dedication to the emancipation proclamation
I'm free and clear but Is clear
really free being a man like me
one may speculate,
walking in terror of a white gown
disguised by a badge and gun
drag and run
loose cases wild goose chases seemingly more times than not
just for a laugh and just for some fun
Tainted Mind...

400 years of buried ancestors turning in their graves
still crying 400 tears daily
rarely is it not about black and white
Martin had a dream of a colorless fight despite
injustices to one group and troops that vanishes in the
midst of a night

anything dark hang and shoot it
hatred for a man of different color skin is deeper than
"deeply Rooted"...
Tainted mind and my walls are painted blind
my colors are clear
I made it kind of like a white boy but fully shaded
or I'm kind of like a black boy but fully faded
color is too overly rated ...
simply stated
Black, white, green and anything that's down or in between
can get sliced and diced from toe to head
and everything inside is just simply RED!

Artie Bryant

18

Illustration by Demitrius Bullock

Walking Enticement

Sometimes I just like to look at you walk,
It could be you coming towards me
or just simply walking away,
During these times I feel
I should just pull up a seat
and just calmly watch,
As if you are on your own personal catwalk
and I am caught up in your hips
and their hurricane
being enraptured in their sexy sultry sway
slowly and seductively
just being blown away,
I just dig the slide in your steps
the grooves in your moves,
To where I am uplifted to a special place
feeling a unique beat
to a rhythm
that only you and I can feel,
Watching you walk makes me wonder
do you actually tickle yourself
with those soft silky strides,
That you are the conductor
of my own personal multi piece orchestra
and with ease
you bring me all on key,
Your walks make me desire to be a better Poet
just so I could simply express
more effortlessly
what it is that you and your walks do to me,
Watching you walk has me enamored
to wonder underneath
what is it that you wear
to artistically capture it all so flowingly,

What choice did you make today??
Is it Panties, Thongs, Boy Shorts, G-String, or possibly
nothing on at all,
When we walk together
I purposely like to let you
get slightly ahead of me,
Just so I can steal glances at your sweet strides
while catching your lasting tasty scent
you knowingly leave behind,
An aphrodisiac trail of where you've been,
Where in the end
to watch you slow your pace
to purposely put us back
in synchronized step again,
To confirm for me
what I already know,
That it's important to you
as well as to me
for us to walk together
to get to where we both wanna be,
Watching you walk in heels
not those beginner shoes either
of 2 inches or lower
that require training wheels,
I'm talking watching you walk
in 3 inches or higher
of heels or wedges,
Though your steps look flawless
whether in flats, flops, or sneakers,
The arch in your feet
the raising of your calves
the firmness of your thighs
to the roundness of your behind,
That creates a hypnotic spell
that leaves me in your trance,
Legs that look like
they could step straight out of yesterday
and still be two weeks ahead of tomorrow,

Because those legs
seem to go on beyond forever,
A walk so unique and progressive
that our ancestors
thankfully because of it smile from the grave,
From the African Coasts to the West Indies,
From the slave ships
to the southern plantations,
Along the Underground Railroad
to the march in Selma Alabama,
From the Black Panther Party
to the never ending Civil Rights,
From the Black Lives That Matter
to the never ending Community Violence,
No matter the reason
I just Love to look at you walk sometimes,
Loving most the walk that takes you
to My Loving waiting outstretched arms,
And after that
the walk away immediately
from our departing Loving embrace,
Watching you walk
carries its own special beat
that no one could ever copy
or even dare try to repeat ....

Poet Crucial ©2018

Jigsaw Puzzle

There is a puzzle that has become undone
ever so often in my life,
It is the same puzzle each time
but when ever it is broken apart
it is never the same to put together again,
And though some things remain the same
this puzzle is Universal to me,
Just as 9 planets revolve around the sun,
The pieces are jagged like fragmented glass
which cut so easily like a sharpened knife,
The hurt that is created once the puzzle is jumbled
is so very intense,
It's a pain that spans a lifetime
if the puzzle is not assembled correctly again,
And as each piece is carefully placed
with the steady hand of a surgeon's pace
back to it's original form,
Each piece reflects the truthful glare of life
so intently that it is felt deep in my soul
which takes me on a melancholy journey,
And as the images brand my mental
as the pictures quickly show,
A sense of self-doubt washes over my essence
and begs me to ask myself,
"WHY?????"
Why waste the time and energy
needed to complete this puzzle,
I already know what the final result will be,
So why should I care?

Especially when indirectly I did not make this mess,
So why does it weigh so heavy on me?
How could one be so callous not to care
what their actions so directly cause,
Because deep down I know,
Just as the sun shares its rays for others to feel the warmth,
I know I must endure to complete this
no matter how much hurt I will face
or tears inside eventually I will shed,
For directly it is me who will allow another
to bask in the beauty of this completed puzzle again,
I must move on and remember not to carry the pain
it took to complete this task,
And eventually the owner of what is now this Jigsaw Puzzle
will one day show,
So I must persevere and correct this mess,
Then shine it up as if it were new,
But most of all in the end,
I must Guard and Protect it with better judgment
against those with weak character
who have false and ill intentions,
With this puzzle
I now struggle with myself to find the love to put back in,
So what is this image
that will reflect so strong and deep
once my puzzle is complete,
In order to really appreciate the sight it will become,
One must be able to respect the value of what it is now,
Even in this humble messy start,
Because the **"Jigsaw Puzzle"** I now speak about,
Are the shattered pieces of my Broken Heart....

Poet Crucial © 2000

Pathways

Love is blind, love grows with a mind
Of its own
Pathways of Love
Eyes, mind, body and soul

Love refuses to live in a box
Each love has a destined pathway that no soul can stop
True love is unconditional with no plans and no plots
Love is mean
Love is a dream
Love is invisible at times
Love carries heartbreak and love is irresistible at times

Love is a bee that hovers with no structures
Lovers fly free and sting unexpectedly
Excessively on the mind
Love is a sea of waves
Sunshine with a sea of rays
Love will always pass any test of time...

Love is a vine
Love grows and intertwines with no sense of direction
Love unwinds when least expected
Love is a blessing
Love last way past the last days
True Love is in the eyes of the beholders
True Love is in the soul...the pathways

Artie Bryant

Piece Of Time

Hey there Queen!
Can I offer you a piece of my mind?
My grind is on a hundred daily
And Rarely interrupted

Time is an invaluable commodity
Time is of the essence
Time is an irreplaceable part of me
my Time is my most precious blessing

Time never stands still
Time is just a simple test
Time will unveil the real
Time will always bring out your best

Time wins, Undefeated
Over and over again
Time connects friends
Time turns something unique
Into something special at the end

We captured this moment in time
Captured it on a rainfilled walk
We Captured it on a bike ride
And some deeply trusted talks

Time heals all wounds
Time is like a room with no walls
Happy that you took a piece of my time
Happy that you joined in the peace of my mind

Artie Bryant

Sorry Love

How do I tell LOVE Sorry
for all the wrong things I did,
Cause see now,
LOVE keeps me at a distance
turns away every time I stare,
Refusing to acknowledge my presence
even at times
when I happen to be standing right there,
How do I to LOVE
make this right,
To be allowed back in the kingdom,
Ending my empty punishment
living in solitude being passed over
from LOVE's harsh banishment,
I'm not claiming innocence
because GOD knows
I'm far beyond that,
It's just that my littered past
of should've, would've, could've,
Tips the scales of LOVE's judgment
showing me now just how selfish I was,
While now serving this time
because of my willing ignorance
from blatantly committing the crime,
I want LOVE
to show me compassion
because now I'm on the outside looking in,
Though when I had it

I wasn't smart enough to respect it,
Always taking for granted
that LOVE would always be there,
I only want now
to bridge this void
between LOVE and myself,
Realizing if she ever rings my phone
I'll be sure to pick up,
Using the knowledge I've gained
during my exile from disrespectful actions
to LOVE in my past,
To appreciate LOVE
for the real gift it represents,
This existence absent of LOVE
is a lonely one at that,
Where I fault no one but me,
LOVE is about possibilities
of what I'm prepared to do
to make it work
if I'm blessed to get another chance,
Not to just talk about it
Because see real true LOVE
doesn't understand that,
It communicates through the 5 senses
with your actions
being the final punctuation mark,
So I hope,
No …
I wasn't hoping when I was living foul,
So I Pray,
No …
I certainly wasn't praying when I was doing dirt,
I just want to believe,

LOVE has not given up on me
during my walk
through this vacuum
of solitary emotional confinement,
Because I've come to learn a truth
which is the first step for me,
After saying "I'm Sorry,"
I just want to work on making it right with LOVE,
Finally understanding unequivocally
unconditionally …
I need LOVE,
Way more than LOVE needs me.

Poet Crucial ©2003

Tentative Love Poem Agreement

Love Poems....
Love Poems....
I was on strike from Love Poems
boycotting the thought of Love Poems,
Because see,
I no longer wanted to write
about a Love I wished to have,
Believing if I avoided Love Poems
making it difficult for Love Poems
to find me,
That only then the realest Love Poem
and only most determined Love Poem
would then be born from deep inside of me,
Because once
a Brother told me
Knowledge Reigns Supreme Over Nearly Everyone,
And that Love is a word
that will get you,
Gotta be careful how we use the word Love
and who & what we use it
to claim Love for,
So I turned my back on Love Poems
no longer wanting to write Poems
about a Love I wished for,
Only Poems about the Love
that finally found me,

So I shy-ed away from Love Poems
purposely turning away from Love Poems
refusing to acknowledge Love Poems
that attempted to rise from within,
And though it hurt deep inside
not to write a Love Poem,
It hurt even more not to have a Love
to write a Love Poem for,
Because every fiber in my being
missed writing Love Poems
even when there was no actual Love
to help inspire the Poem,
It's just that having a Real Love
brings Deep Soul searching Love Poems
and that's the perspective
I wanted in my next Love Poem,
Now don't confuse my refusal
of not writing a Love Poem
with that of arrogance,
Cause see I'm on record of stating
how I realize
I need Love
way more than Love needs me,
Or my Love Poems you see,
So if I'm writing this Love Poem
a possibility of Love
just must be,
I have been told
that when Love hits you
it comes down hard like a ton of bricks,
Making you feel lost
in the emotional heart felt mix,
And this New Sista I met

is currently sending me thru heart felt fits,
She is the vision of sexy
caught up in my head
past my personal defenses
like molecules dancing in the rain
never getting wet or hit,
Images of her consume my being
with sexy figure so clear
that in total darkness
it's her likeness I'm seeing,
Thought provoking discussions of our life
along with rich elevating conversations
dealing with our culture,
Sharing dreams from yesterday
to see if we fit
in one another's tomorrow,
Even embracing the Poetry
of God's written word,
Showing us the internal light
of one to the other
of the Great I Am that exists inside,
Attracted to her sensuality
along with her sexi-ness so sweet,
That I secretly walk slightly behind her
just to taste the air she leaves behind
when together after we cordially meet,
Now I don't know if this means
that my Love Poem strike
is finally over,
And I'll now start writing Love Poems again,
But as long as I have her Smile
in all 5 places
to sign on my Love Poem Creative Contract

I will then openly admit
between her & I
that willingly we have mutually reached
a *"Tentative Love Poem Agreement."*

Poet Crucial © *2007*

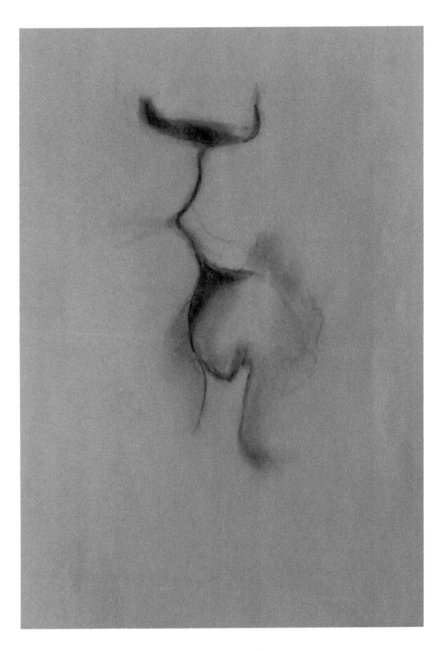

Illustration by Darian Bryant

The Kiss

Matrimony of two sets of lips
Oceans in motion
Sea waves splashing and crashing on seashores
Do you trust your lust?
The Kiss

Lips meet with a touch of tongue
The Magic can flow and both sets can feel the fire
This magical moment could leave you numb
In a split second you will know if you are the one
Letting a guard down in this time of bliss
hit or miss
Shooting a shot is a risk Worth taking
Pucker up…
The Kiss

The taste of lips
Sweeter than fresh berry jam
The firm grip provides a soul security and the safest safety
plan
The Kiss

That tingle in your spine
Goosebumps and your hairs rise
Imaginations do come true
Unexpected foreplay for 2
A true kiss will pierce and penetrate a heart
Like an arrow from Cupid
A true kiss is unlimited to ceilings
A true kiss can separate organic from mixed feelings
The Kiss

Artie Bryant

My Sun

You awaken me with a glimmer of light
A snapshot picture at first sight
We Rise
We Shine
Your rays blind me
My Sun

You watch over my every move
Omni present praying hands
Symbolic with my tan lines Leaving your fingerprints
way beyond mankind's

You pierce my soul to the bone
We have a heated connection
You would kill me If I would let you
Undeniable protection

As you set
The peace and calm overtone is overthrown by darkness
Eventual abandonment by this
Daily apartness

Until you rise again
I patiently anticipate
The warmth from your shine again
My Sun

Artie Bryant

Timeless Kiss

Lost in space
oblivious to time,
Absorbed only by the kiss
with my Lady,
Now that's an action symbolic
of us parting in the park
and as I watch her walk away
as she goes to begin her day,
I wonder if she can tell from behind
that I'm still caught up with her hips
and their seductive sexy sway.
I then begin reconnecting with my whereabouts
and the surroundings of where I stand,
I notice a young boy playing peacefully in the park
with his Grand Mother nearby staunchly watching guard
who in turn catches my eyes,
Now this young boy
was no less than (5)
(7) for sure at the most,
Where once I decided to sit down
on a park bench near
to rest my weary legs,
I didn't realize this action
definitely made me conversation close,
That's when thr young boy asked me
with child curious innocence,
"Mister, why would you kiss that girl like that??"
His Grandmother looked at me with shock

admonishment for him seemingly a definite fact,
But I then smiled in return at Grand Mom
and she then saw it was okay,
I kindly then looked at the young boy
gave a smile and a small sigh
before I then formulated
my hopeful educated reply,
I kiss that Special Woman like that
every day,
Because tomorrow is not promised
something could happen to her today
and never again possibly
may she ever come my way,
I kiss her like that from my soul
hoping with my Love
and these kisses I do atone
to make up for the days
that Love left me so alone,
I kiss her like that for the many Chocolate Faces
who loved and endured for their Black Race
but died before they could see 2008
when a Young Brother
named Barack Obama would rise up
to take our Culture Places,
Becoming the 44th President of this here United States,
I kiss that woman like that
because she is a Strong Progressive Black Woman
representing her heritage
like my Grandmother's, Mother, Sisters, Aunt, Cousins &
Nieces do,
That of a Proud Intelligent Black Woman,
I kiss that woman like that
because I told him

when I was a young boy around his age,
And ignorantly I thought
I knew all there was to know about Love,
And this young girl
then broke my heart,
Stupidly I thought if I offered her 100 pennies
she might decide to give our Love another start,
Had me reminiscing over Peaches & Herb
"Reunited And It Feels So Good"
just wanting her to play her part,
And when my Mother caught me
Heartbroken over this girl,
She scolded I was too young
to be concerned about a girl
and it was my school books
that I needed to be reading and unfurl,
But when she realized
that wasn't gonna be enough
to pick me up out of my funk,
She took the time to come in my room
sit down right beside me to comfort me
put her arms around me,
Where afterwards she kissed my cheek
told me I'd find True Love when I was older
trust and believe in her
one day I'd see,
I kiss that woman like that
for the stories told by my Grand Father
of the strange fruit placed on trees
their lives now never given a chance to ripen,
Or for the women that were raped
having their virtue
attempted to be stolen by the trifling,

I kiss her like that for the times I acted up
And needed a parental kick
because I was young and dumb,
And it was my Grand Mother
Who marched me out to go pick a switch
just to in turn cut my bad lil rump,
I kiss that woman like that
for the children
who have to witness their Mothers
with bruises, blacken swollen eyes, and broken jaw,
For the men their Mother's chose to Love
didn't Love them enough
just to in turn respect God's Laws,
To simply kiss them in return like that,
I kiss her like that for all the Lovers
who are just too afraid
to kiss their own Love's like that,
I kiss that woman like that
so when she is out doing her thing
handling her grown woman business,
And she happens to come across another couple
 kissing like that,
She would never yearn
or desire to wonder
what it's like to be kissed like that,
I kiss her like that because I am Blessed to have her
and I know it,
Because she understands me…
Because she lets me...
And in turn surrenders to me…
Because I Love WE…
And she respects what we are attempting to build
in this relationship you see,

Where after speaking my last word in this Poem
the young boy got up
and kissed his Grand Mother,
His Grand Mother then smiled at me,
And Love
in a kiss that day,
Stood strong in the park
for all who were there to plainly see.

Poet Crucial ©2008

Words Poetic-lee Found

There are times when I sit to write
thoughts are jumbled inside
tripping over the ideas in my head
pushing there way to the front
wanting to be released,
As I format them
putting pen to paper,
Wishing the words that find me
will stop the constant pounding
that reverberates in my mind.

So I wait on words
hoping that when they find me
they will ease the gluttonous tension
that constantly builds in my mental,
Allowing me to find peace
if just for a minute
when I evaluate
the words I regurgitate
that in turn forms the poem
I feel deep within.

I wish for words inside
that will continually move me
to be a better person than I perceive
not to satisfy another's perception,
But to be a better soul inside,
To be a better Father,

A better Son,
A better Brother,
A better Friend,
And one day a better Mate,
Beyond how I see myself
because there is no greater image
for me to impress,
Other than the reflection I see
when I see me in the mirror.

I want the words that seek me
to help me respect
what it is to be sought,
And in doing so
help me to understand patience
better than I did
at the beginning of My Poem
to show me my faults first
before I have the courage
to speak out about another's,
Teaching me to sit with humility
and be silent with myself,
That in time I would learn love
so I could find her
who would complement my ways.

I hold out for the words
that play hide and go seek
only waiting on me
like hot bread and butter
going to get its supper,
Inspiring wanting to uplift
teaching through failures of yesterday

understanding the reality of today
only makes for the promise of tomorrow.

So I write My Poem
with words that come to me
righteous in their origin
true in the end,
As I take time
to quiet the rumblings
from the noise of words
that starts the functional disorder
which perpetuates in my head.

Poet Crucial ©2002

Friend Zone

The fire burned out of control like
Wildfires in the valleys of Cali
Where did my love go?

We talked on the phone for half days at a time
Like teens trying to find love
I knew your words before you spoke them
I knew our bond would never be broken
Heartache and pain in This ocean of emotions
choppy waters and the lonesome is settling in
I'm giving you all of me, recalling we...
Where does this love end?
Begging for your reply to light up my screen
Begging you don't deny my fight for our love and my fight
for my queen...
Where did we wrong?
Please don't prolong, for my heart aches with pain

Minutes seem like hours, no love like ours
Seems like just yesterday when I showered you with towers
of flowers
Please come home, my heart moans for us
Where did our love go?

Her reply defies the laws of love
Disguised and Baptized in the whys
"I love the man that you are
I love the language of love that you express
I love your being and your stance through adversity and
stress...
Our Love is a test and undressed at your request
I love you like a best friend
I love you from now until life ends
But I'm not in love with you"

Artie Bryant

45

Season's Fall

Fall forward towards the falling leaves
Add a layer and ask a neighbor for help
We pray together when the weather weakens
Unified fronts
This is a unique season

Goblins lurk
Demonic themes and scary memes
My Jersey up for my team
Immersed in a cuddle or a no huddle offense
Always prepared
Always ahead

Head to head never stops
Gearing up for Sunday's battles
Are we Living in our future or
Are we living in our shadows?

Jacket and a coat in this season
Bringing people together the most in this season
Hot chocolates with warm
Roasted marshmallows

Mother nature is shedding
Beautiful views
Beautiful times for any wedding
to complete a union
Life's season of recycle
The change is welcomed and
The Fall colors are delightful

Artie Bryant

Marbles For Love

This thing called Love
has me losing my Marbles,
When I was naïve
young and very impressionable,
My bag of Marbles were new,
Full and packed to the top
before I ever recognized
the true value of their worth,
See, every time my heart fluttered
where I was moved
that I felt connected
to a potential female's intimate soul,
I willingly gave a piece of me,
While also allowing her
to take one of my Marbles
from my bag of precious spheres,
Believing my Marbles
would never run low,
Now, after the failed relationships
I have survived,
That in turn taught me about Love,
My heart is now battle tested
and proven emotionally worn,
Carrying scars,
That represented the cracks
I needed to fill,
Then there are the pieces I tediously
had to put back together

after my heart was broken,
And another Marble was eventually lost
for each separate incident,
There were False Loves that came and went
that was confused by lust,
Or where I gave everything I had,
Though in the end
Love was never returned
because there was
No Trust...
No Communication...
No Understanding...
There were those Loves
that tried to reach me
where I was too selfish
to extend a hand back in return,
Loves that were doomed
from the very beginning,
Because though the feelings were infinite,
Their heart
already belonged to another
so I had no business
showing interest from the very start,
There were parallel Loves,
Two entities
heading in opposite directions
from different ends of the spectrum
and only passed one another for a brief moment,
Where circumstances deeper than us
kept us apart,
Each time...
I gave a part of my soul
not to mention

the energy to re-construct my heart,
In the end,
Every encounter cost me a Valuable Marble,
Looking back over my journey
there are times
I should have made better choices,
Smarter decisions
considering now the consequences,
Marbles then
I never should have parted with,
So I need a friend now
one who will openly share
their precious Marbles with me,
While still appreciating
the few Marbles I have left,
For the possibilities of Love,
I have lost many Marbles
while trying to keep my sanity,
Cause hindsight now being 20/20
it was all a learning process,
I'm now just looking
for One Woman,
Who I can give
all of my remaining Marbles to,
And finally comfortably
go crazy for in the end ...

Poet Crucial ©2003

Illustration by Lori Joy

King

A king's walk never wavers
Kings are givers and not takers
A King walks with purpose
A king knows his worth and eliminates what's worthless

Strength and valor
A King brings joy with his smile
A true King spreads laughter
A King's comfort after any disaster

A King's presence
Commands a room's attention
His words resonate and elevate
A King talks without speaking

Sit upon your throne King
Commanding the homage without Demanding
The darts of life protruding your flesh
But the best Kings are still standing

A King leads godly like
His followers never second guessing the lessons
A King Never questions the essence of being his own man
A King walks by faith
A King walks in the footprints already in the sand

Artie Bryant

Faith

Faith is knowing your fate
Without knowing your place
Faith is walking in a trace
Of footsteps in the dark
Faith starts with a tiny voice
"give him a chance"
Faith was written across her breast in the rain
Faith is taking a walk and talk
And looking for nothing to gain

Her voice is music to his ears
Fate is when hearts talk far apart
Faith is closing your eyes
And kissing a stranger On a first date
As the rain drops drip
Rolling down her face to her lips
He catches each drop with his tongue
Is it a moment of love or lust?
Faith is trust
He comforts her soul
she comforts his heart
together Is stronger and longer
Faith always stands taller
Fate is a place of smiles on a studio couch
Faith is the words heard that never left his mouth
Faith is a happy heart when
Uncertainty hits
Faith is a stronger walk when
Adversity sits on your doorstep
For More or for less
Faith is blind at all times but always
Sees clear through barriers and fears

Artie Bryant

Literary Threesome

My Journal, Pen, and I
when together
make an enticing threesome,
Never too far
from the company of the other,
Even when apathy and writer's block
get between us
to try and keep us apart,
They are there always to complete
my final
no matter what Poetic Thoughts,
When not together
I'm on the phone
recording messages that later,
Quietly I'll share with those two,
Willingly I lay
in the pen stained wett spot,
Not afraid to express sentiment
that encourage feelings
to challenge the main stream,
Questioning the obvious
not accepting all that's told as truth,
Rightfully acknowledging wrongs
cause the Righteous realize,
You can't wrongfully get there,
Sparking Passion
to show Romance lives,
Sensually lighting fires

that breathes forgotten hope
back into the word "Love,"
Inciting Rage if Lady Justice
bias-ly removes her blindfold
to tip the scales unjustly,
I so dig this Threesome
that literally flows
when my Journal, Pen, and I
groove together,
A Ménage-A-Trios
of Mental Orgasms
along with Flushed Hearts,
Sweet written elixirs
formed thru
erogenous zones so hott
that whistle
like a ready kettle,
Souls that strengthen
even at times growing wings,
Just from the words
which are products
of the mutually gratifying collective,
This is my writers sordid haven
Where with carnal pleasure
I enjoy always
this blissful Literary Threesome.

Poet Crucial ©2003

If I Could Be

"If I Could Be" that dress you wear
in the Springtime and Summer,
You know the one that sits deep in Slumber
during the cold barren times of winter,
Like the multi-colored blooms that
sleep peacefully in hibernation,
Resting and waiting
for the first signs of the warm seasonal sun
to cascade down on them.

"If I Could Be" that dress you wear
in the Springtime and the Summer,
The one that evokes many looks and stares,
It's made up of 100% breathable cotton,
Its colors and designs are so bright and vivrant
that it could light up a night sky with you in it
as if it were Juneteenth
and not the fourth of July.

"If I Could Be" that dress you wear
in the Springtime and the Summer,
The one that accentuates your body's curves
and flows back and forth, left to right as you walk,
You know the one that looks as if it will rise up
at the slightest touch of the wind,
Dancing at your hem.

"If I Could Be" that dress you wear
in the Springtime and the Summer,
The one you grace
where there is nothing on underneath it,
That dress you wear when the sun sets and falls,
That if one is lucky to catch you
at that perfect moment,
Your sexy silhouette would bear it all.

Please know Pretty Lady *"If I Could only Be"* that dress
you wear in the Springtime and the Summer,
Worn with three inch wedges or heels
that finally accentuates your Figure
that ultimately seals the deal,
Toes painted and out
presenting a total vision
that would make a blind man see,
And make a mute man shout,
See it would then be me that would feel I give you
the confidence and the wonder
to comfortably wear me about.

See *"If I Could just Be"* that dress you wear
that makes you feel you could fly and be free,
Then when the breeze blows and you have nothing on
underneath,
It would be you caressing
and getting close
rubbing only next to me.

Poet Crucial © 2000

Mirrors

Can you see what I see?
Every crack and every crevice
Are you appreciated and loved
Or am I envious and jealous

You look just like me, a carbon copy
Pardon my manners, I'm staring and glaring
You're wearing my clothes
Wearing my flow down to my drip
nakedly exposed
Can you see what I see?

Mask on or mask off?
Blemishes diminished but visible
Complexed and unpleasant
A complicated guy you are
But I'm transparent and present...
Can you see what I see?

Exposed with no concerns of judgement
No worries about any thoughts
He is me and I am him
I can see you clearly
we are ...

Cut from the same cloth

Artie Bryant

Illustration by Darian Bryant

Soul 2 Soul

United on a unique frequency in their own world
Two souls on an organic connection
Their palms meet and eyes greet
With a subtle touch of inevitable affection

Their secret language is a silent fire
Words can't describe this hypnotized potion
Two souls forever entangled
Strangled in a web of parallel emotions

No distance divides this electric connect
Magnets to one another
Permeating each's soul
Anxiously patient for two halves to become one whole

They collide inside like a raging storm
Towering infernos
Lightnings and Aggressive thunders
As the rain smothers and the rain covers one from the other

This fire burns uncontrollable
Soul to soul and flesh to flesh
Checkmate in this game of chess
The electricity of these connected souls can never be
suppressed

Artie Bryant

Interpretations

My erotic illusions
are actual prognostications,
A revelation forged by edification
of my soon to be
intimate declaration,
Though I gave no indication
of my lyrical adaptation,
Just for you
in this poem
I will exercise thru verbal mental demonstration,
Bringing illumination
to all those in adumbration,
Still stuck in emotionless
constipated word deliberation,
What you feel is no misconception,
Sensually Sanctioned....
Deliciously Designated....
A Licentious Love....
That stands the test of time
throughout duration,
That what you hold inside
will always stay true
a continuation of all existence,
Cause to deny it
is to deny me,
Along with all of my mental orgasms
that creates between your legs
the wetness

you actually feel and see,
Which in the end
won't ever allow you to let me be,
So Poetically I wait in Real Time
for your next interpretation...

Poet Crucial ©2003

Brown Eyes Black Heart

Standing in the rubble of My Love Life
symbolic blood stains everywhere
the results of having my heart
ripped from my chest
by the one I thought I would Love,
For the rest of her life and beyond
with only my existence as a compliment,
Now my heart darkens
from the experience of being scorned,
Cold it becomes from failed Love
realizing that all of my efforts
along with my energy
were all for naught,
As the pain inside grows
nothing I do seems to make it subside
moving me closer to a self-fulfilling vibe,
Like a blinded hunter
wishing to quench the thirst for blood
by killing for sport and a mounted trophy,
I too continue my evolution
finding comfort in the shadows
stalking women just for their sex
there emotions no concern to me,
Playing with their sentiment
that now they think they can save me,
Pull me from my depths
and even erase my sorrow,
But my fall is fast in progress,

Though I warn them from the start
about my true lustful intentions
it makes no difference,
My Brown Eyes set the trap
devouring hearts and raping souls
is how I count my success,
Using the tears of those I hurt
to wash their pain from my conscious,
Personal battered emotions darken my heart
which is the only gift I wish to share,
Not caring about the Karma I create
and the day
I will have to answer to it all,
The aura I project now
will eventually reflect back on me one day,
Consequences right now about my future
are empty threats in my eyes,
It's hard to see past the hurt
of My Darkened Heart,
So Ladies
beware of brothers like me
unless selfishness is what you seek
leave me to find the way
from this pain alone,
"Brown Eyes and A Black Heart"
are ingredients for sorrow
in your near future,
If you ignore the warning signs
of a man
dealing with his rejected Love.

Poet Crucial ©2002

Ms. Walker

Our paths cross every early morn
Your smile is as beautiful as the sunrise
Or the natural dew atop the grasses
At times I feel stalker like as
I anxiously anticipate the passing
The moment flashes and passes in the blink of an eye
Barely a time frame to utter the word "Hi"
energy passes through my body like a locomotive
stunned yet another dawn

several days pass with no sunshine
Ms. Walker has vanished in thin air
Fearful that Opportunities are gone for a greet
Fearful that Opportunity is gone for Ms. Walker and I to
meet

my eyes are glued to the ground
watching every step in front of me
At a moment's glance I look up and fall into the most elegant
trance
Today may be the day...

Ms. Walker is walking my way
The sidewalk is narrow
Only room for me and this pharoah
This cleopatra can't hide her joy
She said "Hi" and her voice just echoed

We greet and shake hands
My stomach full of butterflies
a warm waterfall flows in my mind
for A spilt second
Ms. Walker and I connected by design

Artie Bryant

Lost Love

In and out of my life
Dismissive for no apparent Reason
As soon as the doorway of my heart opens
The love is leaving,
You Constantly leave my heart bleeding

Are you afraid of love?
Are you afraid of commitment?
Are you afraid to stay?
Are you afraid of contentment?

You appear when least expected
Space is no qualm
We stay connected
I'm missing my love…

Angel floating with your essence
The presence is impossible to ignore
Eagerly awaiting to restore our love
Eagerly awaiting to hold you once more

Lost love…

Artie Bryant

Insatiable Addiction

That's what you are,
How little I knew then
first time your eyes caught mine
didn't think much of it
at that particular time,
A flirty stare accompanied by a subtle smile,
Looking back now that's when I was gone
ignorant to the obvious,
Me…
Like a gazelle grazing
on the Great African Plains,
While You…
You played the Lioness
stalking in the bush,
Eventually soon conversation ensued
which led us to know
we had so much more in common
on a spiritual personality vibing character
who nourished each other intellectually,
Entangled like a fly
caught in a Venus trap
even still I did not struggle,
Spending time with one another
days on end
lost in your thoughts
and the grooves they bring
like Miles Davis with John Coltrane
playing specifically for me,

Touching your hand
softly gripping your fingers
send shockwaves through me
that warms my body,
Like placing my hand
in an open flame,
So taking my time to caress
and pull you near
slowly we move,
Lost in a hypnotic trance,
Our embrace is purposeful
as our bodies share lovers secrets
which seem over 100 years old,
It's the feeling of Sutra
balanced over perfect Karma,
I guide my hand to hold the side of your face
and then move gently through your hair
bringing me closer,
Enraptured in your fragrance
to sensually taste
your ready sweet lips,
Our tongues probe cautiously
one in search of the other,
It's like venom in my blood stream
finding my heart
Paralyzed and Frozen lost in this particular space,
Compelled to just take you in
time stands still
like a pre-destined moment
meant only for us to enjoy,
Slowly undressing you
as you show the intimate confidence
to undress me,

We anticipate making love
but not before exploring to the touch
feeling lightly with our fingers
and curiously tasting intimate treasures
while along the obvious spots with our tongue,
Desires heat up
creating a passionate swell
like piranhas in a feeding frenzy,
I giving,
Because more you believed
you could take,
You receiving,
past what I thought
were my perceived limits,
Until exhaustedly snuggling
is all we can do,
But after time
withdrawal sets in
my appetite seems limitless,
Once again I look at you
never wishing to do you any harm
and only after experiencing 10 life times
plus forever and a day,
Could I consider with courage
the thought of being satisfied by you,
Because what I see
when I stare at you,
Is my true *"Insatiable Addiction."*

Poet Crucial © 2002

Change For Two Cents

From the first word
to the last thought,
I get lost in the white water
enduring the mental challenges
of this thought-provoking swim,
At times following the blue lines
searching for my Creative release,
Expounding upon visions
caught up in my third eye's sight
that speaks on the journey
which is my Poetic Life,
A witness first-hand
to the stress and strife
reflected in the stain glassed windows
of the many Chocolate Faces
feeling caught up
in this systematic racist economic urban blight,
Young Brotha's
trading text books for guns
the class room for the street corner
the class work for the corner hustle
school for prison
to attain the street life PhD,
Where upon graduation
in today's chilling climate
of 3oo+ murders a year in the city,
Another young man
trades his life for death,

In the never winning gamble
of playing the streets,
Caught up in the Invisible Inferno
believing they have no worth,
The streets have seen many young faces come,
But very few survive,
Too many young folks
thinking they are the exception,
The call of the streets
have existed for generations
with the many numbered revolving young faces
occupying the corners,
Though no matter the alluring life
Prison, Death, & Momma's Tears
are always the rewarding final outcome,
Young Brotha's killing one another
at a rate quicker
than Klansmen throwing strange fruit on trees,
Sometimes over no more
than a stare that lasts too long,
Is this really the lasting legacy
of a young generation caught up
that will define our culture,
As if Willie Lynch himself
is directing my people's plot,
Where the older generation
seems to have lost touch
with the younger generation,
The younger generation
no longer respecting the older generation
and the traditions they represent,
Brotha's disrespecting the Sista's
by calling them everything

but their name,
Exploiting them sexually
to discard them afterwards like trash,
Sista's no longer believing in Brotha's
to lead and cover them like Kings,
A culture caught up in color
where shades and hues
are debated for validation
ignorantly within our own race,
As if being lighter
somehow makes you less black,
And being darker
somehow makes you more,
So please don't misquote me
to take me out of context
and miss the intelligent quotient
of what I'm trying to say,
Because time is ticking for some
and there aren't a lot of tocks
left on the clock,
So make a choice
for there is no middle ground
no gray area to speak of to hide in
when it comes to bettering my people,
Because racist cops await
to erase our proud story,
The past is behind us
which represents our history
and can only be learned from,
The future is tomorrow
which can only be prepared for
like blank pages
waiting to be filled up,

But today is the present
the only moment a gift
that can be currently lived in,
The time now that matters the most,
Where the change made today
with learning from the past
gives hope possibility for the future and tomorrow,
And this is just my Two Cent,
So does anyone have Change ...

Poet Crucial ©2007

Smoke

Clouds gather like poetry in motion
Flowing like liquid
Visibly shifted
Visibly drifting
You disappear and I see clear
Temporarily glaring
Daring to inhale, I'm coughing
Smoke and I
lying in our coffins

Smoke filled lungs and guns
The streets are burning like rubber
The shells whistling through the air
Another summer of alphas wrestling to prove who's tougher
Lives that mean nothing should always matter
Shattered families from just one shot
Smoke hovering around the block like a reaper
Scorned egos like a quicksand that keeps sinking deeper
We all lose
No winners in this game
We all choose choices
The voices claim the heartless sinners in this game
The smoke appears with no limitations or fears
Numb to it as we run to it
Blind leads the blind
behind the cloud of smoke
another mind leaves before it's time

Artie Bryant

Illustrations by Darian Bryant

A Piece of Time

Flying away to a place mentally free
A Cold, cold space selfishly meant for me only
A piece of Peace is solitude in a soulful space
The word deeply embedded in my soul
A Mundane Peace laced all over my face

Life is greater than great
Footsteps in the prints already pre-placed
How great is his grace?

Reasons for his seasons on my lifeline
My lifetime partner
Step by step we are always walking in sync
Peace in my mind He gives me peace when I think

From the Sun, moon and the stars
To The air I breathe
I flow like ocean's waves
For as far
As these eyes can see…
Destined
Through this journey of life
Tested periodically
I'm Lifted with his gifts
His Peace is always a part of me

Artie Bryant

Desired Addiction

This Addiction to Desire
has grown from a small Kitten
to a full grown Tiger on my back,
Where I question the person
who coined the phrase
"You can't miss what you never had,"
Trying hard not to be a dope
but everyday increasingly
becoming a fiend,
Captivatingly caught up
with a vision
seemingly so out of place,
A Country Rose
thriving in this Concrete Jungle,
A Flower better suited
for a dirt mile dusty road,
Petals and thorns
with curves and a figure so thick,
When I stare hard enough
creating a want
in my Desire
that internally just makes me sick,
Like a hunger inside
clinging to my ribs,
Watching you walk…
Quietly feeling your flow…

Reminds me of Gravy, Biscuits
and down home Fried Chicken,
Never even tasted your flavor
have I yet once
to even have a lick,
Lost already in a high
and I'm just only assuming now
what I think you represent,
At this point
I'd even consider rehab
if mentally it would do the trick,
But this is just a crazy Desire
so I'm not sure professionally
what they would even fix,
So I try not to think about it
hoping that would help
my cravings to past,
But withdrawal is a beast
that then starts to kick my ass,
So now I'm not sure what to do,
All of this started from a story
by an Ex in my past,
Can you believe this Sista I'm craving
the cause of this "Addicted Desire,"
Sadly for me is one I've never even had,
So I struggle daily
one day at a time
to satiate this conscious impulse,
Trying to rationalize realistically
from the way
this Sista currently treats me,
That this want is a wish
I will never ever get to have,

So I'm a fiend
fighting everyday not to be the dope,
Chasing behind
a first time never had hit,
Coveting a never before experienced high,
Just trying to overcome
this urge alone Cold Turkey,
It's a burden I carry
this weighted affliction,
Or I'll just call it
my silent *"Desired Addiction."*

Poet Crucial ©2008

Love Ain't Domestic

For this Poem
I want to bleed my pen dry,
Because here in the New Millennium
in a society of change and evolution,
There are current evils at work here
that make me believe in mindset hallucinations,
As if the growth of some men
has stunted and hit a glitch,
Not understanding one simple fact
that any man hitting or abusing a woman
is a Stone Cold Bitch,
Women living in violent situations
dealing with insecure men
that these same women claim as their own
in un-stable un-steady relations,
Wanting to write this poem
for those ladies living in fear
while living also in trepidation,
Swollen Faces...
Blackened Puffed Eyes...
Wired Jaws...
Broken Bones...
Busted Lips...
These are symptoms of the sequence
that leads to a consequence,
Where for most of these women

there is no escape
and the chance for them to get by,
Because in Domestic Violence
 the final result when not checked
is that these women may possibly die,
Realistically murdered
by the sorry excuse for a guy,
The smacks and fisted hits
triple 3 to 1 his apologies
and empty promises to quit,
Murdered by these Weak Character Men
who don't fear sin
or know the Laws of God,
Families destroyed
by selfish actions so tragic,
At times in front of children
scarred images replaying over a lifetime
where mentally for the child creating inner havoc,
Like a Bad Horror Movie
playing on repeat in the mind
not just once or twice
but over the course of that child's real time,
I now stand before you
not as just a Poet
but a living witness,
Seen my Father many times hit my Mother
at times knocking her senseless,
And even as a child had no fear
wanting to protect my Mother
went at him in anger being relentless,
Took my lumps in return from my Dad,
For coming in between him and my Mother
the ass whipping afterwards were certainly bad,

Maybe my efforts were futile then
I was no more
than just young protective and dumb,
But my Mother got away
so she was one of the few Lucky Ones,
And though at times
even now as an adult
the mental replays still spin,
Without question willingly
I'd do it all over again,
To the Men I just say this,
Women can be flip at the lip
talking mad shit
even at times to their man
trying to put their hands on them,
But regardless,
What a Real Man must do
is simply walk away,
Until calmer times come to play,
We men just have to let it slide
or walk away from the relationship
if the alternative is to hit her over pride,
So I have no more words
left for this poem
because I have finally bled my pen empty dry....

Poet Crucial ©2009

Mask

I see your soul
Brown, blue, hazel …etcetera
The depths we see through the unseen
The Eyes of the beholder

I see honor, trust and life
I see a liar a cheater
I see disgust and strife
Mask off

No hidden secrets
I see deep inside
Honesty can't be denied
Pain and anger coincide behind
The mask

Hiding from the mirror
Couldn't be clearer
Anxiety and depression
Peers testing and 2nd guessing
My who, what and where

You stare to see through my mask
But you dare to unmask me
The unseen is pure imagination
Visual images fulfill your conceptual validation

Mask on or Mask off is the question
The answers lie in your own pastures

Artie Bryant

Wet Wednesday

Hump day
Wet and warm just got married
Anticipations for a perfect combination
The love weapons of imperfections

Stormy clouds are watching
Through the eyes of faith and heavens tears are dropping
Dripping down my cheeks
Drops race down my face for a taste
Wet Wednesday

Alluring wet air with a slight sound of rumble
Albany eyes translucent
Albany hair black silk spaghetti
Rain flow glow and Steady

Reasons for this season of Fall
Rain flowers blossom
Pollen wiped away like unneeded rouge
Fall showers grow this secret garden

Her spirit humps mine
Intertwined on this mid-week streak
We speak in tongues just for fun
Valet to my hump day
Wet Wednesday is second to none

Artie Bryant

Empty Feeling

Why is it that I feel so lonely at times?
As if inside of me
there exists a Black Hole,
Which feeds off the love I would give to you
leaving my reservoir of heart felt emotions
constantly seeming drained,
As I sit to contemplate this existence of my world
void of a companion
which I thought was you,
And begin to re-trace my steps with yours
which so truthfully reflect our past,
I begin to notice something now
that was ever present before,
See at times
when we were together
sharing one another's company
or speaking intently to the other,
If our topics did not revolve around you
I stood alone then as I do now,
In my soul I heard music
that I thought was only meant for you and I to dance to
in a melodic whine,
But now looking back
I see it was a groove
that only I could hear,
Because your soul was deaf to this song,
And now that I understand this with better perception,
And I take a closer look
at the footprints inside my heart,
I see that the steps I re-trace
are of me alone walking and waiting

for you to find the inner strength,
To come in and sit down
and walk confidently next to me,
And though I do believe you cared for me
in some way, shape, or form,
I recognize now
the reservoir that once seemed bottomless
where you were concerned,
I needed it to love you
but also to replenish me,
Because in the end
when it was all said and done,
You never cared enough from the start to do it for me.

Poet Crucial ©2000

Expectations

I once told myself
no matter how good things may seem at first
never get caught in *"Expectations,"*
See when you fall for them
it's a cycle followed by letdowns and disappointments,
But Love breeds a sense of belief
and eternal wishful dreams
along with mounting anticipation,
That your heart's true identity
begins to beat through,
Knocking down walls of emptiness
breathing life of warm thoughts
for desire and intimacy
into a place which existed
cold and lonely,
Only True Love with Righteous Karma
can sing the song
to inspire your emotions
to play the music
needed to release your most hidden fantasy,
That place you mentally venture
when alone to be sure no one follows
which details your perception of *"Expectations,"*
Where the thought of just grazing her skin
with my finger tips
sends sensations throughout my whole body,

Thinking of her constantly
day and night
all images except one
cloudy in my mind,
Where it all runs together
like one huge collage
with only her reflection being crystal clear,
Filled with ideas
of where you wish for you two to grow
but yet scared with nervousness
because in truth you have never been there before,
Feeling you must be crazy
when every scent you smell must be her
just when you think
to say to yourself for a reality check,
Am I going insane?
If what I feel is real
then she should sense
I need to hear her voice
and just like that your phone rings,
Butterfly's paired with anxious energy
begin to build
not over doubt of her
because perfection is what she exhibits
like an Angel lost from above,
But from non-belief to know
out of all the people in this world
my soul mate consciously chose
to select and find me
with destiny guiding her heart's decision,
Accepting my shortcomings and what I may not be
intent on Loving me passionately for all I am
while supporting me in what I have yet to achieve,

So *"Expectations"* may seem deep
just take my time I say
enjoy her company in reality
for all the wonders we are meant to see together.

Poet Crucial ©2002

Worky

Breakfast is delightful
Many would call this malicious and spiteful
The 8hour tour
When the 8 skates they both want more
We glow as one for a third of the day
Unconsciously supporting each other
With an unusual nurturing tone
The spouse away from home
The sentence that I start
She finishes
When I'm emotionally diminished
She covers my blemishes
Work wife creates a permanent smile to this work life
We would surely cross forbidden boundaries
If we worked nights
Mid-Day stroll for lunch
Work is nice
We laugh
We smile and we listen
We could be the "IT" factors that each one is missing
Fictional like the owl and pussy cat but we
Expire Close of business
Fantasies and desires of a blanket of kisses
As the workies say "Good Day"
The electricity is undenied
Empathy is in our eyes
Making love sprints across our minds simultaneously
As we say goodbye to another workday

Artie Bryant

Free Friday

Follow your dreams
Soar like an eagle
Or roar like a lion
Never stop trying to explore freedom

Shackled from head to feet
Shackled til I'm dead
I'm Shackled in the head
Still shackled in these streets like an untamed beast

Free is a mind set
Free is not able to touch
But yet still having mind sex
Free is me…

Free is being as vocal as I need to be
Free is being outspoken without feeling broken
I'm free to dream
Free is my life walk and Free is my life theme

I'm free to come and go as I please
I'm free to be what I was created to be
Loving this life until there's no life left
T.G.I.F.

Thank God It's Friday

Artie Bryant

Invisible Attraction

Noticed your beauty
the first time you crossed my sight,
Stared at your presence
when I thought you weren't looking,
Admired your features
from safely across the room,
Blinded by your aura
as it illuminated brightly,
Listened to your voice
and the sweet melody it sang,
Vibed on your conversation
and the touching thoughts you provoked,
Wanted to be closer
but afraid you would not catch on,
Curious to touch
your coco butter caramel skin,
Closed my eyes
to imagine more clearly my distant dream,
Wondered intently
what it would be like to run in your mental
to share your hopes
and protect you against your fears,
Debated with my heart
to question if yours was open to receive,
Craved you so physically,
Wanted to outline your lips with the tip of my fingers,
Pressed for your taste

enough to put my tongue in a few select spots,
Though through all of this
I am not certain you have a clue
cause this *"Invisible Attraction"*
I now do have ....
Is worth nothing unless you can see,
How my essence yearns for you to take notice
and validate my dreams
so that they are no longer just a fantasy,
I now begin my journey,
Adamantly ....
As my mind is now made up
making my way closer to you
by the many people in between,
Your face does turn and our eyes do meet,
Standing in front of you with emotional anticipation,
I extend my hand and say *"Hello,"*
And just hope this attraction is mutual.

Poet Crucial ©2001

Poetic Freedom

There is no place on Earth
that I find
which brings Peace to my mind,
Than that brief moment in time,
When I stand alone to recite
or in front of the masses
my Soulful Poetic Rhyme,
Hoping to touch at least one Soul
as God's Poetic Vessel playing my role
to bring them from
their self-inflicted dark hole,
To know they are not alone,
This is the new age re-gentrification
in this society as I grow & become old,
Where on my Mind, Heart, & Soul
it's starting inwardly
to take an enormous toll,
Cause we have too many Young Chocolate Faces
that are losing their life
in these Urban Gun Violent Races,
So Humbly I go out at night
not afraid of rocking truthfully these Poetic MICS,
Just wanting to open the light
in another's Third Eye sight,
Speaking Passionately from my Heart
about my Poetic Plight,
Using colorful words
thru this gift of Poetry

that represents my simple life,
Hoping I do this with GOD's Blessing
because in my daily Trials & Tribulations
I know he is testing ....."ME"
So until hopefully in the end
when I get to sit next to thee,
I will continue to drop Poetic Rhymes
walking it like I talk it
along this fine artistic line,
Freedom expressed always
when it's Poetry Time.......

Poet Crucial ©2007

Put Me In The Pocket

Melodic rhythm driven
Congos and drums lock it
Once the gogo touches your veins
You can't stop it
Put me in the pocket

Exclusivity to a rare essence
Outsiders unknowingly stop and stare harder
Run Joe Run
Soul searching with Chuck
District's home of Go-Go's Mr. Godfather

Experience unlimited rushing
The funk pouring out of any DMV trunk
Junk and Back yard always pumping
It's Born in the bones
There's No flow like home
Put me in the pocket

Old or new school Kool
Let me clear me throat and flow slow
Hot or cold sweat
You can Meet me or Take me out to the Go Go
Cat in the hat used to do smack
Dropping the boards and the sax
Put me in the pocket
The One on one
Jack and Jill going up the hill to have a little fun
Trouble dropped the bomb on your crew
So scream it the loudest
Now tell me where yaw from?

Artie Bryant

Freedom Ring

Let freedom ring as lady sings the blues
Freedom screams
When Freedom Sings
Freedom has a Dream
Freedom sits on a throne alone
How can a man like me be free?

Skin colors divided
Brothers decided Freedom is only determined
By cheaters disguised as leaders

Married to free
Til Death do us
Back of the bus sodimized and
They feel compromised sitting next to us
I'm Free from hate today
Never Freed from the barrel of a .38 today
The White sheet removed and some replaced by blues
Choose with no choices and lose by fate today

Leaders will always lead
the rest will have a need will follow
Making America Great Again
Incarcerated souls in black holes
This old "great" is an
impossible pill to swallow

Thou shalt not steal
Or kill
Constitutional rights were written in a bill and
8 more commandments demanded that these be
Written in Freedom's will

When will freedom sing?
When will Freedom start freeing all beings?
I want to fly Free as a Bird
flying high in the sky
I want to be Free like clouds that levitate for miles
Let Freedom Ring

Artie Bryant

Illustration by Demitrius Bullock

Juneteenth Celebration

Fourth of July
and again for another year
You Lie,
July Fourth is not My Cultures
true Independence Day,
That holiday for people like me
that share My Melanin
is forever June Nineteenth,
Our legal freedom came in Texas
two and half years
after the end of the civil war,
Which many in My Culture
bled and fought for
then eventually also died for,
There were no rockets' red glare
or bombs bursting in the air,
No freedom for us to share
though many had been brave,
A large population of My People
were still considered slaves,
And even when freedom …
Freedom finally became certain,
They made sure to let us know
we were still beneath them
to only write us in
as $3/4^{th}$ of a person,
So how could freedom embrace us
when still so many of us
were broken and hurting,
Only when finding our own
could we then break free
from the racist seeds that they sowed,

Fourth of July
and again for another year
You Lie,
July Fourth is not My Cultures
true Independence Day,
That holiday for people like me
that shares My Melanin
is forever June Nineteenth,
And until it's finally seen
as the National Holiday
it deserves to be,
I'll personally take that day off
to celebrate with my people
whose past history agrees with me,
Never to forget their blood also
originates from the Red, Black, & Green
just like me,
Now I'll also still enjoy being off
on the Fourth of July,
But for a different motive indeed
because My Freedom
was officially secured
on what we Love as *"Juneteenth,"*
Though still now here in 2020
there are basic liberties & rights
afforded to others
that's not afforded to me,
Or those whose skin color
is dark & rich like me,
Fearful still of a modern day lynching
by the kkk
disguised as the modern day police,
Along with those deputies in main stream amerikkka
willingly playing their part
against us by calling those same police,
From the racism steadily growing
that was sown in their hearts,
So don't speak to me

about some Fourth of July
because then again for another year
You Lie,
Since July Fourth is not My Cultures
true Independence Day,
That holiday for people like me
that share my melanin
is forever June Nineteenth,
And again still in 2020
under this 45thth President
of these divided states,
I'm fighting for a privilege still
that you are given
just by being born with pale skin,
And if I was afforded
even a thousand extra life times
each time without doubt
I'd certainly always choose to come back as Black,
To Celebrate True Independence
with My People
whose melanin glowed like mine,
Understanding the Importance
of finally being free
on this Day *"Juneteenth"* …

Poet Crucial ©2020

Scent-full Thoughts

Smelling your personal fragrance
no matter where I turn
overloading my nasal senses,
Existing all around
permeating through me
driving my sense of smell crazy,
Forcing me to re-arrange my priorities
making finding you
the top task on my list to complete,
As time moves on
the more of you I seem to inhale
which has anticipation
kicking patience to the curb,
Creating an insatiable fiend
that intensifies my Loving hunger
to lead me to want to devour you
and satisfy my carnal addiction,
It all started,
The moment you exited my bed
in your essence you left behind,
Covering My Pillows,
My Sheets,
And My Comforter,
It's a sweet trail
that had me toss and turn
to begin my quest,
Of finding the treasure at the end

which is you,
Your image firmly embedded
in my thoughts,
As I get dressed
your scent wafts softly
from deep within the fabric of my clothes
bringing me to remember
your fondness for wearing my things,
Though the harder I press to find you
the farther it seems my journey becomes,
Making me inquire to myself
"Are you a want? A need? Or a desire?"
In conclusion I realize
your karma encompasses all three,
Because from the things you do to me
the way you treat me,
Holds my mind hostage
where I would gladly pay your ransom
and give you my heart,
Where my search is draining ...
The pursuit exhausting ...
I travel until I can go no further
to where returning home is all I can do,
Arguing with my soul
about the fruitless efforts of my search
along with the un-quenched thirst
for you I long to drink,
Only after turning the key
to enter my place
do I find the most intense scent
of you roaming all around,
Which leads me to my bed
and the un-real sight of you,

Smile on your face
arms out stretched
as you embrace to pull me in,
It's the subtle whisper
of your voice I hear last
"Oh! How I have longed to get back to you,"
Which puts my spirit at ease
to know this desire is mutual.

Poet Crucial © 2002

Free Minds

Retired minds writing words
That inspire
Your views are higher
Then the sun, moon and stars

Freed hearts on similar pages
Freed lives in Similar stages
Time is limitless
We never know how much time he is giving us
Free your mind

Spread wings and fly high
Shuck and jive talking
Many souls in the universe
Just dead spirits calmly walking

Shining lights in dark places
March forward with a smile
And no dark traces
Free your mind
Closing all closets
And freeing all basements

Free to grow
Free to flow without restrictions
Free your mind of all convictions
Free your mind
and a freed mind freely listens

Artie Bryant

Lifesavers

Lifesavers in all flavors
Placed in the path of life
Lifesavers for all occasions
Lifesavers for listeners and lifesavers there for advice

Pillars of healers
The angels of life
The savers are changers
In the most difficult strife

The life preserve hurled in the 12th hour
The prayer responder with more than prayer power
In desperate times
The Lifesaver never waivers

The bravest moments require hope and faith
Your lifesaver
Your angel that's present in every space
Your lifesaver
Your angel that always keeps everything safe

Your presence is always felt
Uplifting and never shifting from loyal
You are my lifesavers
Braver than you know
When my saver is needed you faithfully always show

Artie Bryant

Wishes

High Imagination,
Marinating Day Dreams,
My eyes passed a note
your smile checked yes
whether standing in reality
or floating on my sub-conscious,
It's the aroma
of your familiar scent
that leaves a lasting impression,
Taking my time
to carefully pick and sort
through all that does not belong
Slowly, as I get to know you
accepting totally the good and bad
of all that is left,
There are those who claim
they definitely have better,
While others do covet
what I wish to call my own,
So no matter
their unwanted perceptions,
Wanting to inhale you
is all I really desire.

There are times I call
just to hear your voice
not that I want anything
it's more about

wanting to know you are there
to listen to your soothing melody
because when I have you,
I can never get enough of you
like an *"Insatiable Addiction"*
eating away at me from the core,
And when you are around no longer
I yearn to be in your presence
dancing on the positive karma
you unknowingly leave behind,
A trail from one person to the next
as I follow aimlessly
drifting over to the left,
Understanding if I had to live
all of my days like today
without you in my life,
I would rather wake up to yesterday
eyes wide with anticipation
just to have the hope
of knowing you might be in my tomorrow.

I look at you
with nothing particular on my mind
just mentally sketching your image
so when I am alone at night
surrounded completely by darkness
my heart the only beat I hear,
I vividly replay your picture
believing one day
soon next to me you will snuggle,
Where in this mellow haze
cloud nine is the lobby
the only place to go is up,

Experiencing your mental intimacy
feeling the heat from your body's pulse
shows growth from my heart's past,
So sit and share with me
exchange stories with our true self
which brings realness
of all we have in common,
That together we see higher than my imagination,
And marinate sweeter than my daydreams.

Poet Crucial ©2002

Illustration by Darian Bryant

What If Poetry Was A Crime

Living in a world constantly on edge,
Every day now
seems like the brink of destruction,
People in a rush to see the final days
as if we ain't already moving there fast enough,
Bodies falling in these streets
like rain drops from a turbulent thunderstorm,
Kids killing one another
like it's some new age childhood generation game,
Blood now coats the asphalt
making crimson the new aged paved color,
Politicians elected to be leaders
to make life better for the people
seem to only add to the decline,
Lining their pockets
to compromise their office,
Auctioned off to the highest bidder
to eventually sell their soul.

So to My Poets & Poetry Lovers
I ask You …
"What If Poetry Was A Crime?"
Dropping Metaphors
Speaking Similes,
Meant for Poets to do

actual hard time,
I mean if that was True
would you as a poet
really renounce your gift,
Or would you like me
understand the life saving mentality
of spitting these phrases of poetry
that allows your Soul to be free,
If I could be so bold always
not about what I've been told,
But what I feel deep inside
when it comes to this Poetry,
Painting pictures with words
that if you closed your eyes,
Tickling your senses
to where it's about what you hear
as well as what you see,

Enough to smell, taste, & feel my Poetic stories,
For I am Poetry
and Poetry is definitely me,
I would gladly be wanted
by authorities
at the risk of doing a bid,
Because when it comes to this Poetry
this isn't some fad
but in real how I live,
These Poetic stories that I write
contain parts of me
that speaks about my life,
I need this Poetry in order to survive,
Because without this
written and verbal art

deep inside I'd certainly die,
So if shackles and chains
along with a 6 by 9 foot cell
was my fate,
I'd write and run
and run and write
easily without question
for the rest of my life,
Stand the man down
in the face of incarceration
especially when the alternative is
to give up my poetry,
Treat him just like
Sheriff John Brown if I was cornered,
"I Shot The Sheriff"
And if I had to
I'd even shoot the deputies.

So To My Poets & Poetry Lovers
"What If Poetry Was A Crime?"
Dropping these adjectives
Speaking these adverbs
colorfully using words,
When as a Poet
if I was caught,
It only meant in the end
I had to truly serve,
Well I intend to go out on My Feet
and not on my knees
because I wasn't raised to be scared & a coward,
I'd still talk about Big Brother yall
that's the "G" to the "O" to the "V"
along with the apostrophe "T,"

See that's the conservative curve
that continues to keep my people down,
Minds still shackled 400 years later,
So their Bodies have no choice
but to physically still in bondage,
Where mathematically thru legal means
they attempt to keep us on a string
playing us like we're puppets,
Dance puppet dance,
That's the system y'all,
Without fear or hesitation
continuing to speak from my heart,
Because Unconditional Love is still limited
between us
in this world we currently reside,
So I ain't turning my back
on this gift
flowing thru me from the Most High,
Smiled on additionally from above
from assuring fiery eyes
standing by the Most High's
Right Hand Side,
By living Righteously,
Hopefully…..
They all will save a place for me
in the Most High's Sacred Kingdom,
Then allowing Me to Rock HIS Open MIC,
Cause the New Prophecy
talks about the Poetic Prophets,
Bringing a message
we have to seriously be about
doing more than just talking
not afraid of the walking,

Because I come from a Culture
that is descendants of Kings
a heritage to rich to ignore,
I'm not that ignorant nigga
that main stream amerikkka wants me to be,
Nor am I a hitting Women Mother
that my Father exampled me to see.

So to My Poets & Poetry Lovers
I ask You,
"What If Poetry Was A Crime?"
My blood line is that
of the Anunnaki,
For this gift of mine
is that of
Heaven to Earth,
Only negative thinking
along with a selfish weak ego
with the Devil's guiding
can miss-lead me,
From this Poetic path
it's already destined for me to walk,
Cause with this gift
I true thee must speak,
So whether I'm caught
or not,
Or read it in the papers
or maybe see it on TV,
Don't worry about Me
because even locked down in a 6 by 9 foot cell,
My Mind …
My mind always will be free,
Because in the end

I know
only God can ever truly judge Me,
Even if this right here,
Poetry ….
Poetry was ever even truly considered a crime
in the end.

Poet Crucial ©2006

Dream Queen

Reminiscing on the first look
Seeing glee in her eyes
Disguised and guarded
Fearful of a scarlet impression

Every kiss has a meaning
Dreaming now and then again
Anxiously awaiting when
Anticipations on a visit from a lifetime friend

Patiently awaiting when...
Penetrations to her mind, body and soul
Patiently awaiting when...
We purposely lose control

Dreaming of her heavy breathing
Dreaming of her laying on my chest
We are making passionate love
Yet the foresight of a car ride with laughter resonates the best

Dream Queen
Ultimate aspirations
Father: I'm asking for patience
Destine for our paths to cross
Our love may be invisible
But Our love is never lost

Artie Bryant

Hard Rain

The sweetest joys blossom from the hardest rains
The darkest pain is seldom invited
Years of tears and fears
Unconditional loves are seldom divided

The soul delivers the messages that we are too blind to see
Insecurities from a past block the blessings we are trying to see
No blockages on this journey
No blockages from what you are trying to be

After the rain
Life's a sunny, warm place
Petals
Laced with love
Love's levels uncertain and dubious

A protected heart projected the march
Will be isolated like a life of an only born
Aftermaths of the soul that's torn and scorned

This palace is sacred
Emotionally naked
Impossible to fake it when your spirit is shaken
Impossible to fake it when your heart has been taken
Hard Rain

Artie Bryant

That Woman Poetry

Emptiness with nothing
is the feeling I hold
when paper is before me
pen available full of ink,
And blankness is all that comes out,
It's a darkness created
from a void left open
when my Lady Poetry disappears,
It's an indication
that my situation stagnates,
Currently adding up to zero
when mathematically tabulating
thus far my completed written prose.

See Poetry is the element,
That woman that balances
my emotional sanity,
Allowing me to find
the proper words
description defined clearly
via the correct adjective,
Poetry helps me to express
that what I deeply feel inside,
Pushing back the vagueness,
Making Clarity ....
Relating Intently ....
Connecting experiences

in her sensual deliberate intoxicating way,
Which sets me free
that breaks the mental grip
apathy once held
on my literary essence.

She supplies light in understanding
guiding in its brightness,
Conveying melancholy when I feel sad,
Feeling happiness when I have joy,
Evoking anger when I witness injustice,
Providing a stage for me to perform
when I'm falling deep from love,
Or quietly teaching me patience
when things don't go my way,
I Love this Woman Poetry
realizing she is a God given gift.
It's only her
who can fill this blankness
though right now
she is no where to be found,
I love her freely
with an open hand,
Cause she belongs to me
while I am dedicated to her,
So when the time is right
the moment conducive for listening,
Poetry will whisper in my ear
directing my right hand,
Colorfully providing the poetic pieces
I now share,
Since we last spoke.

Poet Crucial ©2003

Cipher's Effect

When the Cipher is in Effect
the verbal flow is percolating,
Charging electricity to my brain stem,
Neurons then start firing
mentally stimulating the mind,
The pages in my journal
then begin to itch,
Forcing my pen
to start scratching
with ideas formulating
deep from inside my head,
Just letting my thoughts go
in the presence
of a Poetic Collective,
Or silently alone
writing within
my obscure creativity,
Then when ready,
Sharing these stories
to the congregation
as I light up the mic
with tight moving musings,
It's like
passing around the collection plate
not for anyone
to put anything in,

But hoping it's my clear message
poetically they will pull out,
Riding an Artistic Wave
that to the straight analytical
they just can't feel,
Cause the current
from the left side of my brain,
With its pull
is just too deep,
Either you get me
or you drown,
Mild Mannered…
Laid Back…
No need to show off
the phat "C" branded on my Poet's Spirit,
Unless just artistically needed,
And that represents
the creative *"Crucial"* prose
for those wanting to know,
But really too afraid to ask,
This all happens I remind you
when the Cipher is in full Effect.

Poet Crucial ©2003

Illustration by Darian Bryant

Dark Ghost

You appeared one year and never left
Unexpected ghost close to my heart
You and I will never part ways
My dark ghost present on dark days

Multiple stents meant to keep you away
persistent and never distant
Driving the lining of my highways
Down for a ride like a Queen and Slim or a Bonnie and Clyde

You take my breath away
Forceful like an untamed boa
This match is forever ongoing
This match is forever growing

I walk every step with you always near
Once feared but now I love you
You keep me awake and clear in the here and now
I will Never succumb or run and never throw in the towel

For we shall continue this life path hand in hand
Step by step exam for exam
My Dark Ghost always close and ready to show
But you imposed on an uncommonly strong man

Artie Bryant

2020

2020 hindsight
Would have done it all over
Shoulder this pain with no closures to gain
2020 surprised me
Where is the love?
Beings dropping like flies
Death is among us

Will god step in and end it?
The curse for the worst scene
Quarantined to city limits
a shitty pandemic, how did we get in it?

Helpless days and nights
No vaccinations
A deadly dirty bug
Surprise attack on this nation

Misinformed calculations and accusations
Desperate applications for a cure
2020
Monstrous and heartless
Anxious for your departure for sure

Black lives matter
But kneeling hurts feelings
Opposite spectrums of perfections
We're all singing a song that's all wrong
If A nation's fate is solely decided by a nation's election

Artie Bryant

Communicating in a
Third Eye Language

It's… It's… It's…
A Verbal Conversation
of Mental Stimulation
conducted on a Cerebral Plain
that Physically only we can see,
Where in your eyes
I see possibilities
beyond vivid images
of the Hope you place in my dreams,
Speaking on the dilemma's
facing our people,
Along with speaking on the inspiration
And truth revealed from deep inside,
From this country showing their reaction
of when a Black Man resided in the White House
as the 44th President,
From the African Coasts
to the Slave Ships
thru the Middle Passage,
To the auction blocks
where our people were sold
families dis-oriented and broken apart,
Strange Fruit on Trees…
Plantations…
The Under Ground Rail Road…
Emancipation Proclamation…
And our Civil Rights…

126

Where this Son
would understand his Father's Lack of Love,
And this Father
wouldn't worry so much that his Son
understands his Love,
Because the Sins of the Father
can grow to be Sins of the Son,
Where young mis-understood boys
wouldn't grow to be frustrated grown men,
Education would be the foundation
making employment to empowerment the reward,
And Gun Violence
wouldn't be the choice as Judge & Jury
 in our community in the end,
Women respected for the Queens
that they represent
like ancient ancestors back in Kemet,
Never abused or treaded upon
covered like they should be
where LOVE is Real,
This we speak about
without ever using our voices,
Because understanding with us
is Crystal Clear,
You and I
communicating in a Third Eye Language
where when I stare long enough,
You have me to believe
that We….
You and I….
Could take on the world
and without question most definitely WIN,
Now maybe this all sounds like game

just some smooth Poetic Talk,
And if so...
Let me state now as a Poet
understanding the Power of Words
if it's ever proven I was false,
Let it now be considered the 8th Deadly Sin,
Because this Poetry I speak
is True recordings
of our Third Eye Meetings,
Where It's... It's... It's...
A Verbal Conversation
of Mental Stimulation
conducted on a Cerebral Plain
that Physically only we can see.

Poet Crucial ©2007

Forbidden Fruit

From the very beginning,
I knew I was in the wrong
even before we ever conversed,
Saw her in the corner
dancing by herself
just as sexy as she wanna be,
Now I should have known
no way in the world if I was single
this woman would ever approach me
in the manner that she did,
Direct and to the point,
Cause you know the saying
when you're single
they are nowhere around,
But become involved
and they come in swarms,
But that was the problem,
See I wasn't single
had a Righteous Sista
at home solely in my corner
being supportive
making it all about us,
I tried to play uninterested
repeating to myself,
I have a woman …
I have a woman …
Seductively,
This sexy dancing vixen

slinked her way over
made herself comfortable
right next to me,
Extended her hand
told me her name
said *"Hello"*
all with a sly smile,
With caution I stuttered hello back
while gazing
at her perfect quarter build
she was worth two dimes and a half,
Right here I knew I was in trouble
because I was no longer pro-active
just re-acting to her to stay afloat,
After some conversation
she told me she made a decision
and now was ready to leave,
Told me I needed to make a decision too,
Then I thought
just because she would let me
does it make it right that I should,
I thought about my Lady
one last time
and the heartache this could cause,
Fearing the power
of a scorned woman's tears
or the pain of their sting,
Psychologically this woman's sensual ways
was trying to play me
from inside my own head,
Wanting me to play Adam
to her Eve
enticing me to partake

of her Forbidden Fruit,
And risk being kicked out
of my woman's paradise forever,
Trust her, she said,
No one will ever know
this secret we share tonight
it stays strictly with us,
Blindly I followed
being led by my other head,
Caught up with this Siren's alluring song
leading us to intimacy
where I lost my moral conscious
and the fact
I had a good woman at home,
We did the do
I enjoyed the deed,
Just as I was finding comfort
in my dishonest deceitful stand,
I heard a key in the door,
And this Forbidden Fruit
covered her mouth with her hand
cause she never warned me once
that she lived with a jealous
non-trusting man.

Poet Crucial ©2003

Faithful

Met this woman with upright respect
for my Poetic Art,
Who had devoted intentions
to negotiate truthfully
for my constant Poetic Heart,
But even before I ever said a word
she laid out honest measures
from the very start,
Rules and Guidelines sort of
she stated in a promise
that she would never thaw-art,
Acknowledging that she understood
how Poetry loyally was my first Love,
And never would she attempt to compete
in my life conscientiously
with that sacred part,
Just asking me staunchly
after all the time, performances, & enthusiasts
did I understand and know *"Faithful"* with clarity
enough to be emotionally smart,
Now with my attention captured
on such a unique initial proposition,
I contemplated carefully inside
about my own personal perception
of the *"Faithful"* definition,
Where my fickled past
of false partners

brought to light my faithless relations,
From traitorous women
filled only with unstable motives
lined with treacherous intentions,
And in that moment
her understanding for the Love of Poetry
that dwelled deep inside of me,
Opened me up without question
to free me mentally,
Like an Epiphany…
That verifiably…
My Heart and Soul could do nothing
but simply just follow,
For *"Faithful"* is a reward
rooted in the incorruptible
when the foundation is communicated clearly
as well as finally factual and just-ly,
"Faithful" knows just as in Life
death is certain to follow,
"Faithful" is a Loving Parent
that after watching their child falls
still unswervingly will always be there
to brush them off
and again help them stand tall,
"Faithful" is the character of a Culture
that from the slave ships in the Middle Passage
to the oppressors stinging whips
not to forget the hard fought Civil Rights tip,
Believing in a Dream to overcome
while watching a Black Man ascend
to become the 44th President,
All the while as a steadfast Sista
had his back,

"Faithful" is the Love I have for this Poetry
to write my mind and my emotions free
even as negativity and hate
attempt to falsely cloud my sight
so in my third eye I won't see,
"Faithful" is taking the Righteous Long Road
respecting my Family and Ancestors
for the short cuts just don't last,
"Faithful" is life's education
I never stop learning
or otherwise I'll never get ahead,
Respecting in Life
there will be definite storms
but if I quietly hold on
trusting God to guide me,
He will replace those storms
with rainbows in the end finally instead,
"Faithful" understands
with each grain of sand
Father Time controls the clock,
So I can't afford
to waste remaining time being unhappy
then my Balanced Poetic Peaceful Center gets docked,
"Faithful" is the Father who stays
when he becomes a Dad,
Maybe not with the Mother
for this I am guilty of
and some considered it bad,
But most certainly the child
this I knew,
Cause we have too many Single doing it alone Mom's
and that's a predicament
for our race that's extremely sad,

In the race to claim Young Black Males
between College, Prison, & The Graveyard,
The statistics are harsh
with Colleges & Universities
losing the battle at an alarming rate,
And just when I knew
she understood my perspective
on a level communicated that between us
at that moment grew,
I took her hand
accepted her resolute offer
and told her with these words
as a Poetic Black Man,
"Faithful" are my final actions
of how I'll always be to you
because on you I would never give up,
Realizing finally with you
I could never trade up,
Beyond the Time I give to Poetry
the Performances that grip the audiences
and lastly the Enthusiasts who afterward
felt my Poetic Vibe,
I will always have "Timeless Kisses" of affection
mixed with thought provoking
"Poetic Chocolate Injections"
for finally between You and I
"Faithful" will always be our connection,
This I give as my example
of my "Faithful" to you.

Poet Crucial ©2009

Illustration by Demitrius Bullock

Keeper At My Brother's Side

Good Brother ....
My Brother ....
Born from the same Mother
whose blood flows Red, Black, & green,
We have always been connected
through our melanin
attached to the same team,
I was there beside you
when we were both placed
in the bowels of those
over- crowded slave ships,
Arms and legs chained
forced to sail hip to hip,
As we both watched
When the slavers threw over board
our siblings who couldn't
survive the arduous trip,
Through a Middle Passage
that was the start Our Cultures
Rites of Passage,
That we have since endured
for 400 plus years,
Where today still
unjustly our brothers
are savagely placed in early caskets,
From the slave masters whip

to the task masters grip
a history in this country
outlined by a brutal trip,
Documented in our history
by the Strange Fruit that hung from trees,
Through the fight for Rights
we already knew wee Civil,
They called us Nigga
to ensure we would know
we were not their supposed equal,
And sadly today
we still play the unwanted part
in this brutal atrocious sequel.

So Good Brother ….
My Brother ….
Why in an age of Knowledge & Information
Some of us still willingly
call one another Nigga,
Then feign righteous hypo critic anger
when another culture does it
I see that logic as quite absurd,
Centuries later
some still playing the ignorant part
of mindless sheep
just following the herd,
We are born from the Original Culture
nurtured by the First Mother
to walk this planet,
Her blood flows Red, Black, & green
And always I've been by your side,
I was there when Willie
also Lynched his divisive seeds

amongst our people
those roots sadly still holding strong today,
I too am the un-ripen product
from a Father with Mother Problems
and a Mother with Daddy Issues,
I wasn't fortunate
to be born with the Vision and Knowledge
to immediately be qualified to carry the Righteous Hammer,
But with Time, Education, & Patience
we all can evolve to carry the weight.

So My Brother ....
Good Brother ....
We have to start by respecting each other
to stop killing one another,
Support, Protect, & Uplift our Sista's
by being the example
of Rectitude and Responsibility,
Exemplifying Fairness
to Honor their presence by our side,
Raising our children together
so they would understand
to learn True Love & Virtue
in our melanin,
But some of us still
reluctantly or fearfully refuse,
So they leave our strong Queens alone
to carry the burden on their own,
But always through it all
faithfully I've been by your side,

Only needing you to turn your palm over
to find my reflection

in your black hand side,
Instead some among us
insist on remaining at odds with one another,
Fighting to break up
and continuing to fracture
our beautiful proud tribe,
As main stream amerikkka
delights in our division
sending their Racist Political Officers
to pick us off one by one,
Until all of us as Buffalo Soldiers
are finally done,
So instead of pushing back
to fight the oppressor
with a unified Black Fist,
We bring the frustration home
to unleash on our Queens & Kids.

So My Brother ....
Good Brother ....
Always know I've been here
carrying too the scars from the whip
bruises from the police man's baton tip,
Nursing wounds
from the police man's dog bite,
Soothing the wounds
around my neck from the noose
which gripped so tight,
And through it all
they still have not drenched my fire to fight,
My inner strength is determined
to always stand by your side,
A desire burned through manifestation

from their downright hateration,
Even today they still kill us
in broad daylight
trying to instill fear,
And after my eyes sweat
to shed a sorrowful tear,
I rise so they will learn
I ain't going nowhere,
But even more My Brother
I want you to see & know
that by your side I'm still here.

So Good Brother ....
My Brother ....
I say this now openly to you,
As long as GOD opens my eyes
and the Universe allows me to simply breathe,
The blood that flows through me
is that of our ancestors 400 plus years ago,
A heart that pumps
to an Ancient African Drum Beat,
Then I will tell our stories
through this Poetic Heat,
Hoping it will resonate
long after I am gone
to inspire one to put it on repeat,
So whether it's these Poetic MICS
or Racist Officer Political types,
They are gonna always get this lyrical work,
So just know
I'm here to lean on
standing by Your side,
As we share this melanin

we have no choice but to ride
as long as it's a Just & Righteous Vibe,
To support our Queens
and uplift our Community.

Because Good Brother through it all
you will forever be My Brother,
Born of the same Mother
whose blood flows Red, Black, & Green,
Until the very final end ....

Poet Crucial ©2020

Heart's Uncertainty

They say Love is forever,
See, when your mind is messed up
you can see a psychiatrist,
When your spirit is weak,
Accept Spirituality,
Fall to your knees
and talk with GOD,
But when your Heart's Uncertain,
Floating around in limbo
trying to find
steady ground to stand on,
Cause the love you felt,
You thought was certain,
And no matter what anyone
tells you right now
you just can't hear it
their words deafened by your pain.

Now spending time with yourself
after your love wounds have healed,
You find your heart
in a directionless numbing journey,
Destination is no particular place
except not to go back
from the pain it just came from,
Deep in your heart lives,
This feeling that just sits,

Waiting....
Wanting to find
its equal feeling partner in return,
You know that part of you
where your heart
is so willing
to give this euphoric pleasure,
Just needing only to find
someone worthy of this gift,
This is when your true self
debates with your uncertain heart,
Sometimes,
With a cloudy judgment,
Where the definition of Love
and what you wanted,
Was crystal clear.

Though during this uncertain fog
sincere principles of love are tested,
When it all clears
and your heart
is no longer uncertain,
What will matter most in Love?
In this brief moment of life,
As the last days are falling,
Will your love be based still
on Sincerity, Truth, & Honesty
along the path
of a righteous exclusive union,
Or have you given up
thrown in the towel to quit,
Because your constitution is weak
and you don't hold the fortitude to endure,

Maybe lust has taken over?
How about Material Love?
Will that matter more
than emotional commitment,
Would you allow your heart to darken
to poison other hearts
that you wanted to intimately
come in contact with,
Those that were single,
And even those that were committed,
Because hurt people hurt people,
Just know the Karma's energy
you now give off
will eventually one day reflect on your soul.

See, I believe in Love still
along with the simple principles
it represents to me,
Just someone genuinely I dig
willing to fight for us,
Pay the price of happiness
for my Love I give unconditionally
while in return
only asking for the same,
So maybe right now
my *"Heart's Uncertain"*
with no sense of direction,
But every day with time,
It does get a little bit clearer...

Poet Crucial ©2002

Images To Truth

Illusions create images
that perpetuates perception,
Forgetting facts
that show off Truths,
Cause some would rather swim
in a diluted reality,
Believing their ignorance
grants them plausible deniability,
Refusing to consciously recognize
the questions that sincerely need answering,
Ones that could bring direct clarity
to the vagueness
we willingly manipulate,
Instead,
We avoid acknowledging the ambiguity
holding it all in place
with our self-imposed tainted honesty,
Then we judge others
wanting to believe
someone else is guilty
for the pain we will inevitably feel,
When actually,
We were running from the hurt
before this current moment started,
Self-Inflicted is this agony,
Blaming it on someone else
is the weakness of our character,

Finding courage
to ask the hard questions,
Removes the darkness
to shed enlightenment,
Self-Introspection....
Brings Accountability....
When we are honestly open
to the true self answers
of our self-questions,
Not twisting the results
to what we want them to be,
Cause only then
after destroying perception,
Will images fall from illusions,
Leaving only the bottom line,
That finally we see honestly
the open truth
that reality brings.

Poet Crucial ©2003

LOL

Letters of love
Imaginations untamed
Attracted to her flow and style
Ms. Beautiful, "What's your name?" with that sexy smile

The elegant image
 she's winning
Can I have an appointment on your calendar?
Lavender is her escape
warmth flows with her essence and grace

her innocence is pure and a tad shy
can't deny her alpha
she listens to her intuitions and complies
even her shy is sexy and fly

one kiss is worth a million letters
whisper her words of wisdom and words of pleasure
cherish her treasures and seek spiritual porn
not so much secularly physical, let's connect in a mental and
lyrical form

torn between flesh and blood
letters of love
her voice is a melody telling me all I want to hear
let me jump into your pool of love with no reservations and
no fears

Artie Bryant

Prince George

Mr. George
Royal and plush
Kingship at its finest
Your highness, the royal flush

Full menu Tulsa continued
Home is where the heart is
No boundaries in this county
Chocolate pouring out in all flavors

You are beautiful and an abundance of pride
A ride through empowers me
You shower me
With inspired intentions of ambition
Mr. George's soul food for your cultural nutrition
PG's pedigree better be staying determined
Stay churning the wheels of success
Passing all test
Prescribed Suburban if you have a love for learning

Multitudes of diverse dispersed
Throughout your square footage
The thirst for purpose is second to none
Impactful of black and how great this black has become
No other space like your palace
Your fingerprint thrives in every arena
Filled to the rim with self-wealth
No limitations
This is Prince George and no imitations

Artie Bryant

We Didn't Say Goodbye

Only if one more masquerade
One more Christmas party
If we had one more Halloween dance
If I only had one more chance
We didn't say goodbye

If I could hear your voice once more
What would I say?
If we could just play one more board game
What would we play?
One rematch on the tennis court,
But I'm sure I would lose once again
If I could have one more glass of vintage wine
just one more conversation
with no obligations ….
We didn't say goodbye
If I could have one more hug and one last kiss on the cheek
Just catch one more glimpse of your hair blowing
As your convertible rode down any isolated street

You are the candle that shines in your circle
You are the inspiration that will live in us eternal

You left a void that will never be filled
The lives you touched loved you so much
I'm beyond blessed that we met and until we meet again
I will carry your smile as you lay to rest …

In Memory of Joni M. Coleman

Artie Bryant

150

Ujima

She asked me my name
while I was deep in thought
staring out the window
thinking over the things
my life's journey has taught,
But then slowly
I moved from my deep state
and her face & appearance
I finally caught,
Curiosity got the best of me initially,
To where I blurted out innocently,
Do You prefer Sugar in Your Grits??
So quizzically she looked at me,
Understanding the expression
my question had wrought
in her eyes,
The answer I sought I told her
was buried deep within her
Mentally & Spiritually ...
Her full attention
I had now bought,
Told her personally
I prefer butter, cheese, salt, & pepper,
But Sugar on Grits....
There is a disposition worth truly considering,
My Grand Mother & Mom used to stress
you better eat those Grits
they stick to your bones
to help you endure life's cold hard duress,
So this is the time of Kwanzaa,
"*Ujima*" the principle of today
to address,

The Third Principle of Collective Works,
Togetherness on matters of common interest,
Because your problems are my problems
and my problems are yours,
And only by building together
can we survive & solve
these hardship life tours,
So when considering the Grits
we mix up for life's bowl
please put some Brown Sugar in mine,
To help me survive #45
and his unfair racial stance
of main stream amerikkka
with their gender bias
and whites only times,
Cops killing unarmed blacks
openly crossing righteous lines,
Judges handing down unequal sentences
to those whose skin color
resembles mine,
And we've started to become numb
to these socially racial crimes,
Even More ...
They are openly killing
our young children
as if we are blind,
So I don't know if you can tell
but my Soul hurts
my Mind is wrecked
and my Heart bleeds
in these rhymes,
Just wishing for some Brown Sugar
to now put in My Grits
to stand by my side
and hold me down,
Coming home to her always
after enduring the day
of facing these tribulations,

Allowing her
to help rebuild my strength
and re-energize me
as I do the same for her in return
so I can continue to fight these situations,
Because my problems are yours
and your problems are mine
so only collectively together
are the solutions we find,
This is when I then noticed
how this Sista was in tune with my words
and she was without question definitely a dime,
Here is when my stance started to soften,
Recognizing her strength and beauty
because rarely if ever often
am I captivated like this,
I simply then took a deep breath
extended my hand and said...
My Name Poetically is *"Crucial"*
But You ...
You can certainly call me *"André"*

Poet Crucial ©2019

Sista Flavored Chocolate Ice Cream

Chocolate…
HHHhhhmmm, that's my favorite,
Tasty to my mouth,
Smooth going down,
Stimulating for my mind,
But see if I'm not careful
sure to catch a brain freeze,
Chocolate Sista's…
You have to appreciate
their many different shades
from one far side to the other,
I in turn Love them all
no matter where in the spectrum
their Chocolate Flava may fall,
See…
On one far side
 you have Chocolate Chocolate Chip,
A strong dark flavor
tantalizing to the taste,
While on the far other side,
You have Chocolate Vanilla,
A creamy mixture
of a softer flavor
but just as deep to savor

for the tongue you see,
Then there's Chocolate Mint,
Chocolate Swirl,
Chocolate Fudge,
Oh my goodness
how I Love the taste
of *"Sista Flavored Chocolate Ice Cream,"*
With so many different flavors
of Chocolate available
out here for you to taste,
How can one not be enticed
to wanna have a scoop,
They talk about Brotha's
selling out at an alarming rate,
Well... Hey...
Don't get me wrong
I can appreciate other flavors,
And the possible uniqueness to maybe indulge,
But see I'm NOT God
so I am not fit to judge,
And in the end
who knows what Flavor
Real Love will finally take,
But to give up on my Chocolate Sista's,
Man you must be crazy,
In the words of Flava Flav
before he became commercial machine of today,
Back when he was down with Chuck D
the S1W's, Professor Griff, Terminator X, & Public Enemy,
"Don't believe the Hype,"
Have you checked the ingredients
of the natural essence
that True *"Chocolate Flavored Sista's"* hold,

No preservatives allowed,
Sassiness in her attitude,
Where the mounds of pleasure
in her curves and appearance
seem to melt just right,
There are so many different Chocolate Flavors
out here for one to taste,
I have not even begun to name them all,
But one thing is certain
she is not meant for the weak stomach,
Because that cat
he is sure to be Lactose Intolerant,
This Chocolate dessert
is meant to be had
by only one strong individual
who can appreciate the joys
of tasting
a *"Sista Flavored Ice Cream,"*
She will stand alone though
for as long as she has to
until just ONE Righteous Brotha comes along,
One who can digest all she represents
while ingesting her Sweet, Sweet, Sweet Chocolate ways
inside and out
enough to enjoy her fully,
Now if I have gotten this far into the poem
and you have no clue what I'm talking about,
Let me be the first to tell you
I can't help you,
But if you feeling me
as well as vibing on my words,
Digging this poem
and my rhymes

while appreciating my poetic lines,
Then that means one of two things
you have either had some
"Sista Flavored Chocolate Ice Cream"
and for some reason you lost her
so now you are fighting
for all your worth to get her back,
Begging for a possible *"Second Chance"*
at something
you probably wasn't even worth the first chance to get,
Or you currently still have
Your *"Sista Flavored Chocolate Ice Cream"*
and you are holding on to her for all you are worth,
Realizing what you had
you would crave no other
by always making sure
to lick your bowl clean,
So I just have One Question
before I end this Poem,
Can I have some Ice Cream??
But make sure it's *"Chocolate Sista Flavored."*

Poet Crucial ©2002

Creative Muse

I have a serious issue
this problem persists
since I lost my *"Creative Muse,"*
I'm just not the same anymore
filled now with emptiness
of thoughts I once had,
My *"Creative Muse"*
slowly sexed my mental
leaving her subliminal orgasmic cream
embedded deep in my subconscious
that in turn left my head gratified,
Which in turn helped me to express
to you
my deep true unspoken words,
Speaking to me with compassion
feeling the power of looking in her eyes,
Where consciously,
I tasted her honey filled scent
felt her sensual touch,
It reminded me of my very first
intended passionate kiss,
See my *"Creative Muse"* was free,
She taught me about Love
in a way without using words,
Making the fear of emotional heart ache
non-relevant in my soul
in this world today filled with so much hurt,

Intimately she freaked me
engulfing my manhood
with soft tender loins
that was only rivaled
by her warm inviting mouth,
She only touched me
with intentions to leave it on my mind,
So I could learn to appreciate
the sensually Loving vibe
of a inspiring *"Creative Muse,"*
From Sunrise to Sunset,
Twilight till Dawn,
I would search high and low
to find this precious gift
I once had confidence
to call my own,
Willingly see,
I'd change religions now
and you know how some
are serious about their religion
if it would allow me
to open her mental presents of orgasms once again,
But see a *"Creative Muse"*
she floats like the wind,
And only if she wants to
will she ever come my way again,
Though now I have nothing
a void vacated by her obvious absence,
I no longer have her
to safely tuck me in at night,
Wanting in anticipation
just one more time,
To hear her whisper to me

intimate progressive poetic thoughts,
That were secrets once only meant for me to feel,
Cause in truth they were too deep
for her to just captivate with plain simple words,
So now abstinence is my fate,
Not willing to taint her memory
with just any old passing thoughts,
To those who can relate
if you see my *"Creative Muse,"*
Tell her I asked about her
hoping all is well,
You don't even have to tell her
about this poem I did tonight,
Because since she has left my mind,
Writer's block has been my company,
Leaving my pages to remain blank,
And my pens stagnate full of ink.

Poet Crucial ©2003

I Used To Love Her

"I Used To Love Her,"
Love Her like a Country Girl
who loved her fried chicken, grits, & collard greens,
"I Used To Love Her" Mind
how she always made me think
like I was caught up
in a deep game of chess,
Just wanting to solve the puzzle
and not become lost in the scrabble,
Hoping to always find her in the end
like hot, bread, and butter
coming to get my supper,
So I could stay warm to hot in the end,
"I Used To Love Her" Curves
because if I wasn't smart enough
to wear my seat belt
she was sure to throw me for a loop,
"I Used To Love Her" Lines
deep enough with strength
forcing me to always hold her hips
at the required 10 and 2 position,
Or certainly I'd crash into the wall,
"I Used To Love Her" Hair
allowing me to pull it
because their roots were buried deep
across the ocean
in the soil of the Mother Land,
Curls so strong
I could spend days
running my hands through it,
Never getting lost

or losing my way in her jungle,
Always a sense of which way to go
to find my way home,
"*I Used To Love Her*" Voice
The sound she gave
was that of a morning sunrise,
Enough to make a hurricane
come across as a summer drizzle
a tornado
like a light spring breeze
a tsunami
like a quiet sunny day at the beach
"*I Used To Love Her*" Walk
with style and flow
as if she could hear music
like Marvin & Stevie
at an old school block party,
Like her legs were the pied pipers
you couldn't help to be caught up
to follow them wherever they'd go,
"*I Used To Love Her*" Eyes
I could see my image reflected
so deep in them,
They were like Truth Serum
falling into a trance
I'd willingly tell her
whatever she wanted to know,
Just hoping she realized
and knew deep down I'd never lie,
Eyes so telling
they showed me easily my future
one I couldn't imagine
without her or them in it,
"*I Used To Love Her*" Lips
the ones upstairs
as well as the ones down low,
The ones up top greeting me like a morning dew
on a sunny perfect day,

Tasting like fresh picked cherries
to where hours later
I'd lick my own lips
in hopes of tasting her again,
The ones down below
seemingly smiling at me
when I turned my head slightly to the side,
Like crushed fresh peaches
when I worked my tongue just right,
Would never consider shaving the hair on my face
because sometime later
I knew if lucky
it would hold her special feminine scent and flavor,
"I Used To Love Her" Complexion
the shade of chocolate
mixed to perfection,
With just the right amount of caramel
so with the sun's reflection
cascading off her skin
that perfect golden hue
would push right on through,
Her perfected skin tone
showed the Zulu Warrior
deep in her,
And the Kente Cloth
that held it all together,
"I Used To Love Her" Soul
and how at one time
she freely bared it all to me,
How our souls danced as one
to the same deep African drum beat,
Sharing the parts
others couldn't handle
a truth openly we accepted,
Inspiring Poetry deep from within at times
while she danced a realness
only to be seen in my poetic lines,
"I Used To Love Her" Heart

and all of its imperfections
it carried from failed past attempts,
She made me feel comfortable
to offer mine
in its once broken state
that I carefully pieced back together,
But now her heart no longer
belongs to me
as she callously dropped and broke mine
like a parried move,
Which ends up
being a heart broken burden
I'm now forced to carry,
Because in Truth
"I Used To Love Her"
and that realization in the end,
Is finally no longer scary to me.

Poet Crucial ©2018

Illustration by Demitrius Bullock

A Too Real Nightmare

As a Black Man
have You ever watched
a Black Woman Cry,
Over the pain caused
by a Black Man's lies
that she openly allowed in
to let get close,
Where with each lie he told
she believed it for Truth
unlocking doors inside
that further allowed him in,
To play her mind
while getting closer
to her Soul & Heart,
The epitome of the 8th Deadly Sin,
The Melanin in her skin
only served to add flavor to her cries
tears filled with color
born from his blatant hurtful lies,
A wound of treachery
filled with deceitful poison
infecting her blood stream
to finally blacken her heart,
To a point that for safety
she believes for her best interest
forever from All Black Men

she must finally emotionally part,
Can You imagine the depth
to wounding a Sista
that logically in her mind,
For her to heal
this is where she believes
she must start,
To genuinely Love a Black Woman
requires Patience & Truth
which is a sincere acquired taste
of honest fruit,
But when fellas refuse
to cherish the precious gift,
Then the divide between
Black Men & Black Women
becomes an uncross-able rift,
Forcing us to watch
from a distance
as another Man from another culture,
Provides the Love & Support,
She first sought from her own
to finally experience
her emotional felt lift,
So can us as Black Men
really fault her
for her growing weary
of her heart being treated
like a *"Jigsaw Puzzle,"*
Some game being played
to see how fast
we can put it all back together again,
After casually attacking her heart
with that Male BS

from the start,
Continued Deception & Evasion
to begin,
How many more tears
will she be forced to shed,
From the falsehoods
derived from a Black Man's Head,
Why must the thought
of a Good Black Man to some
be a Myth or Illusion,
To afterwards make a Black Woman
feel for safety that she must run,
As if the thought
of a Righteous Black Man
who is both Protective & Supportive
is some far-fetched myth,
I can no longer handle
seeing our Beautiful Sista's cry
from Black Men
who only know how to lie,
But before I can speak on it
from the outside,
As a Black Man
I must find my own Black Queen first,
Then be the example
to live it Righteously
on the inside in the end ...

Poet Crucial ©2020

First Born

We missed many moments
That are not retrievable
Agreeable that life must continue and the foreseeable
Future is an anticipated welcome

I didn't teach you how to tie your shoe
I didn't teach you how to ride a bike
I didn't teach you strength through times of feeling blue
I didn't teach you skills about life

I didn't find you nor was I trying to
I am guilty for those dismissed actions
Life happens and many times comes with regrets
Life happens and many times there's no resets

We met in your adult years
Greeted with many adult tears
Time can never go back
We can never retract the steps nor the whys or why nots

Emotionally filled past tense and I try not
To hinder the progressions
Lessons learned and lessons earning
Burning my resentments with poetic confessions

Let your eyes look straight ahead son
For too long these words have been unsaid
My son, I'm proud and speechless
A man's apology is never a sign of weakness
Love You Son

Artie Bryant

Letter To My Son

I remember your first cry like it was yesterday
I held your fears and tears with a firm grip
Vowed to see you through your bad to better days
I stand as a proud father in every way

My little "bop" into a grown man
Stand strong son
Storms will always arise and due time places them behind
you
Every life has obstacles, but none can confine you
Not a day went by without a ball in your hands
Not a game went by without your pops shining with pride in
the stands
Always the shine to my dark days
I Pray that I didn't pass down any of my dark ways

A man in every sense of the word
I seek your leadership as these tables turn
I give you the baton on this life trip
You are captain now of this father / son life ship

It's hard to explain the happiness and peace gained from
fatherhood
The most precious gift received
I relish in joy with all that you have achieved
Son, I Believe in you

You remind me so much of me
I blush at times as I see in every angle of you
there is a touch of me
From boy to a man I am lucky dad
Now we walk as men hand to hand
Love you Son

Artie Bryant

Illustration by Darian Bryant

Letter To My Daughter

A princess is born
Full of joy, smiles and her own style
My forever needed lifeline
You gave me life at the right time

My mini me at any and all times
My "wildfire" down for any ride
I knew the day you were born
Your tiny hand in mine, I vowed to never leave your side

Missing you 10 times more than you can ever be missing me
cherishing the Priceless memories that you have giving me
From birth or a tee Ball fail in the dirt
to traveling this earth and a broken nose in Tennessee

My original "hoop-star"
Now my life saving angel
My heart is forever indebted
Our father daughter love is forever connected

Blazing your trail in your life walk
You make me proud to be your dad daily
The life of any and every event
I admire your fortitude and your inner strength

"she got Game" and my Hawk will never die
My unconditional Love for you princess D
can never be denied
YOUR FATHER WILL ALWAYS BE BY YOUR SIDE!

Love You My Princess

Artie Bryant

Heart Sick

I have an illness
with no known cure
except for time,
Slowly eating at me
from the inside of my heart
throughout my whole essence,
Only time will tell
if this sickness will get the best of me,
Barely I hold on it seems
from one day to the next,
Hoping that tomorrow
will be better than my today,
Searching for the faintest sign
that I may make a healthy recovery,
Enduring my symptoms
cursing the pain I wrought
feeling for any who have suffered my fate,
That the Love they loved
is no longer,
My heart stumbles
over this finite ending,
I am reminded everyday
of my unhealthy state,
Whether it's an image of a stranger
presenting a likeness I knew once deeply
from a love soured
seemingly just yesterday,
The urge I feel

to say your name
in hopes of it being you,
To feel the warmth of your smile,
Depth of your hug,
Or passion in your kiss,
Just once more
locked in a moment of eternity,
All I have now are memories
which run 24/7
like an emotional movie marathon
where I am helpless to stop the show,
Catching the smell of your scent
even though you are nowhere to be found,
As though the wind carries you
from all four corners of the Earth
with the space I occupy
the center of the breezes destination,
Like a kiss you would blow to me,
Conjuring up secrets between us
that I struggle to shake,
Dealing with my sickness
thoughts I will have to let go of
if I am ever to heal properly one day,
Not succumb to my fading situation,
I have to accept
what we had is no longer,
What I am left with
is an illness deeply heart felt
that one day I will get over,
Though only through time,
Only through time …

Poet Crucial © 2002

Poetic Intimate Thoughts

Waking up out of my sleep
in the middle of the night
to start writing a Poem
about this Sexy Female Poet,
Whose words resonate
in the walls of my chest
and settles finally
in the pit of my stomach,
Whose physical images
kidnap my day thoughts,
While still strong enough
to hold my night dreams hostage,
Yet,
It seems I'd have a better chance
to possibly capture smoke,
Or even strangle water,
Then I'd have to get close to her,
To inhale her sexxxy feminine scent
or simply digest her grown womanly essence,
To only then regurgitate it
so I could willingly digest it again slowly
a second time all over again,
Savoring her every taste
kissing her lips
with intense true dedication,
And it doesn't even matter
which pair it is,
As long as when I'm done afterwards
glowingly with honest satisfaction
genuinely they would both smile,
You make me want to sign my name

all over you
claiming you as my very own,
Carefully writing my name
meticulously in hieroglyphics with my tongue
in the form of sweet kisses
all over both sets of your lips,
Tasting your tongue,
While engulfing your clit
with my initials,
Carefully writing *"Crucial"*
on one side of your inner vagina walls
with my unique tongue's spin,
While signing *"André"*
on the other side
with My Natural Chocolate Pen ...

Poet Crucial ©2019

Natural Hair Crowned Royalty

Have you ever seen
a Woman of Color
regally rocking her crown,
Now before I get started
let me just say,
No matter how this sounds,
This is no slight
to the Women of Color
who enjoy wearing
wigs, weaves, and extensions,
The choices you make
is all about personal preference
your own inner to outward description,
But to My Chocolate Beauties
who wear their hair naturally beautiful,
Whether
Kinky, Nappy, Twists, Loc'd, Afro, Bald, or even Permed
as long as it's originally yours
born from the scalp,
Then this Poem Queen
is definitely about you,
To me there is nothing more captivating
than a Woman of Color
rocking a Majestic Crown
of Beautiful Natural Hair,
It seems in today's world
so caught up in Superficial Appearances
catching a Woman wearing her own
forces me to take notice
to simply stop and stare,

The way her crown
dances in the gentle breeze
just riding the season's air,
Watching her from a distance
as she freely with ease moves about
maybe carrying the weight of her world
without an obvious care,
I so badly wish to run
my fingers through her illustrious mane
my desires I'd lay bare,
But since she is a Queen
I humbly need her permission
otherwise I wouldn't dare,
Wondering the scent of her tresses
their softness to touch,
Her demeanor aristocratic
placing my feelings in a rush,
Curious if her commanding look
is strong enough to pull or grab
through intimate curiosity
thoughts to maybe make her blush,
To me there is nothing more elegant
than a Progressive Sexy Woman of Color,
Wearing her Own Magnificent Natural Beautiful Hair
as the noble crown it is,
Just watching it bounce
or just watching it lay,
As I watch you float
as you seductively walk away,
Your hair just flowing
leaving a mesmerizing trail from behind,
The imagery is hard to properly define,
I just hope that in this Poem
with my folliculed rhymes
I do your regal hairdo justice
and my truth is kind,
Because if I could
I'd certainly be your King

and you along with that hair
would forever be mine,
Yes Indeed
a Woman of Color
rocking her own natural hair,
There is no better vision
one I see as fine,
Because a Black Woman
without question in my eyes
is already a dime,
But one who rocks her own
draws me in like a straight line,
That if I couldn't have you in this life
I'd dream every night
in hopes of a chance
for you in my next life time ...

Poet Crucial ©2019

Night In Paris

I want you like a *"Night in Paris"*
on *"Juneteenth,"*
More than I've ever wanted
anything in my life
to find comfortable sync,
When I'm with you
our souls connect
like we've done this before
over many past lifetimes,
It's just the way our spirits link,
As if everything before you
in my life was brief practice
lasting the time of an instant eye blink,
The Jones Girls once sang
about *"A Night Over Egypt,"*
When I was misled
I thought Janet, Sade, or Halle
was my desire,
Though after spending time with you
lost in your mental company
you definitely now make My Heart believe,
Not only just in things I feel ...
But also the things I see
as well as those things unseen,
I hear you in My Head
talking to me when physically
you are nowhere physically around,
Then when in your physical company
and silence between us
is the dominant sound,
Mentally connected we are

that loquaciously in our minds
thought changing world conversation
comfortably abounds,
Yeah I want you like a *"Night in Paris"*
on *"Juneteenth,"*
Where the images
of a righteously committed mate
you plant the seeds of belief,
That if I was Blessed
to endure & see
a thousand lifetimes with you,
Just in one of them
I'd hope to be worthy of you,
As you claim always to me
I repeat back to thee,
You inspire for me
to aspire to be
the conscious better version of me,
To finally just once
see the day
the Universe would reveal to me,
I am equally deserving
of all you have to offer
to form a better stronger we,
This union of ours
is divined from Love's Pure Way,
Where I'd chase you
over infinite lifetimes
like the moon follows the sun
or how night chases day,
I would hold you down
when life's tribulations tested you
support you when life's trials
tried to knock you,
Pour nothing but Positive Karma
into you,
Breathe nothing but Love
in My Kisses to you,

Replenish your strength
and fighting energy
with my very own if I had to,
I want all of our evenings
over eternities lifetime
to be Our Special *"Night in Paris,"*
Like Unrestricted Freedom found
on Our Own unique *"Juneteenth"* ...

Poet Crucial ©2019

Summer Love

The other day I believe ...
My Forever Love
sent me a small clue
that she might return my way,
Had me reminiscing about a time
when she was the center of My Life,
She left me close to a year ago
leaving me to suffer
in a cold colorless place
that cut like a sharp knife,
The Smiles in her absence
were far and few in between,
Our time together
never seems to last,
No longer than 5 months if that,
Though during that brief period
her warmth radiates
touching my skin
to heat my core
leaving my soul to smile,
When she is around me
she kisses my heart
that lubricates my joints
to help me move effortlessly
and face the questions of life,
Her presence is so True
that she easily effects all
who are caught up in her company,
Willingly they would openly
bare their skin
just to in turn
feel a small part

of the fire she brings,
She would gladly be the reason
I'd keep her over all four seasons
for multiple lifetimes,
When she is in my life
my sleep is peaceful
my nightmares nonexistent,
My days are longer
the smiles are endless
sharing tasty water ice
which only makes our bond stronger,
I wish I could hold on to her 24/7 for 365,
But I guess in order
to live that life,
I'm required to move
to a place of warmer climate
where Summer results are plentiful
and definitely rife,
So no matter the season
Summer will always be
my very First Love,
The female sights she inspires
during a Warm Summer Day
are mostly right,
Even after the sun sets
the Summer brings
beautiful star filled nights,
I'm faithful to Summer
so even if she only stays with me
5 months a year if that,
I'll endure the time
she stays away,
Because I know in 7 months or so
she will finally return my way,
My "Summer Love" ....

Poet Crucial ©2019

Cold Toes or
Two Comforters

It's a faint feeling
though enough of it though lingers,
To remind me quietly
that once it was here,
Now without its presence in My Life,
I'm forced to sleep with Two Comforters
during the cold nights,
Or I suffer to wake up
with Cold Toes in the morning,
When it was in my life
this problem was never an issue,
I'm talking about that Black Love....
More like the Black Ice
you never saw coming,
Though once you were on it
you knew it was real,
Keeping me warm,
The flava of Mocha Supreme
Mixed down like in my Hot Chocolate,
I don't drink coffee
just for that simple fact of reason,
Cause the residual effects to me
makes me too jumpy plus uptight,
Her brown skin in memory
was the vision of Chocolate

laid back for ever just smooth,
Mental Intellect
cruising with Sophisticated Progression,
Carrying the history
all plus 400 years' worth
of our Culture's Oppression,
Even lined in the footnotes
plus scattered in the margins
it was filled with the many Brother's
who could not love their Mother's,
So how could they ever
know your value
to in turn appreciate the gift you gave,
Your Black Love ...
A body with figure so deadly
to false prophets,
But the secrets of her sexy Figure
Was like sailing the Middle Passage,
But one you would travel in reverse,
Knowledge known
to the one she anoints
to these special secrets,
Navigating her body
was like Euphoria,
The Prodigal Brotha's & Sista's
going back home,
Sailing from the Omega
back to the Alpha,
Her feminine essence
with all its abundant riches
represented the Mother Land,
I would make Love to her
multiple times a day

just so afterwards I could catch
the Sensual Scent
every time she left afterwards,
Smelling like
Sweet Royal Egyptian Musk,
Where the temperature
because of her presence,
Never dropped below
12 Noon in the Nubian Dessert,
Now seemingly seasons away
in another lifetime,
All I have are distant fading reminders
that are falling too far in my past,
And I fear one day I wake up
these memories are disappearing way too fast,
And finally one day I'll wake up
these memories will no longer last,
Cause I sleep now
with Two Comforters
during the cold nights,
Or I suffer to wake up
with Cold Toes in the morning.

Poet Crucial ©2003

Could We Be

Could I be about you
you be about me
having us be about it together
so that we could just be,
Beyond the reasons we see
as obstacles that stand
before us,
Past those around us
who silently hate on us,
Interjecting their unwanted neg-a-tiv-i-ty
trying because they have failed
so they attempt to keep us separate-ly.

"Could We Be,"
Bigger inside
than the hurts we feel
that no one else can see,
Ignoring the past unknown list
of others who thought
they could be in our lives
regardless of how long
that line may possibly be,
See, cause I'm feeling you deeply
past those warm eyes
beyond you're seductive smile
through those protective feelings
that guard your heart
where you in turn deeply feel me.

"Could We Be,"
Compassion to each other
feeling a connection
that pulls us to one another
like a child to presents
on Christmas morning,
You remember that feeling
deep in your stomach
racing down the steps
to look under the tree,
Only with this,
Replace it with us,
Where it could make me silent
years at a time
all in hopes
of just hearing your heart beat.

So *"Could We Be,"*
Cause hope guides me
to believe that
you endured to find me
like I held out
to eventually find you,
For we were meant to be,
So let us get together,
Finally,
To just be ...

Poet Crucial ©2003

About The Authors

Poet Crucial

Where do I begin, when speaking about Me, *"Crucial."* A Poet who is Blessed each day I wake, at another chance for Me to get it right, and even more to write about My Experiences, My Journey, My Life, My Truth whether Good, Bad, or Indifferent. *"Poetry is Me, and I am Definitely Poetry."*

Initially, I wasn't comfortable enough to share My Poetic Art publicly, but the gift inside of Me was becoming stronger every day, to where in My Daily Routine, I always needed to write, or had a deep urge to create via Pen and Paper, in the form of a Poetic Prose. So write is what I did, filling up My Journals with My Poetic Perspective, but it wasn't until I met this Progressive Woman named Ms. J. Dean, and within our relationship, as our feelings grew, and trust between us became strong, to where I trusted her in My Place alone, and like any Woman I guess, she started to check things out when I was away, and she eventually found My Poetry Journals, and once she started reading My Poetic Stylings, she became My Number One, and Only First Real Fan of My Poetry, and she continually pushed Me to get out and check out the Poetry

Venues there in the City of Philadelphia where I resided then, with hopes of encouraging Me to get up and perform in the end.

But in time our relationship ended, but her support for My Poetry never wavered, even after we broke up, to just become friends. And if you ever heard that saying, *"When one door closes, another door opens"* ... Well, that's what happened.......
I found courage finally, with the end of our relationship, to follow up, and see where this Poetry could lead Me, or even if My Talent was worth sharing. So I started to check out the Poetry Venues in Philly, still wouldn't sign up, but at least finally I was out there following My Poetic Compass. To where finally I signed up on the Open-Mic List to perform at WarmDaddy's, which was being hosted by Warren Oree, and The Arpeggio Jazz Band at the time, but it took Me until My 3rd time coming out, before I was finally called up to perform by the Host, and from there it has Been On!!! Which led me to *"Panoramic Poetry"* sponsored by the October Gallery, *"Blue Funk"* and performing there, Thanks Johnnie B., for giving Me that chance, to represent on the same stage as one of My Poetic Idols, Mr. Gil Scott Heron that night. Then *"Jus Words"* @ Dowling's Palace, Nexxus Gallery with The Heat, *"Word 4 Word"* @ Art Noir, Poetry @ Third World, *"First Friday's"* with Sista Azziza, *"Zion Train"* @ The Pearl of Africa... All Beautiful Progressive Positive Venues in Philadelphia. Not to mention being fortunate to travel outside of PA, to other states, and parts of the Country, even to the Caribbean, where I have been asked to perform My Poetry. In addition to opening for the Legendary Gil Scott Heron, I've opened for Dr. Sonia Sanchez, Musical Artist BlackStreet, Jaguar Wright, Lady Alma Horton, Carol Riddick, Les Nubians, & Overseas Artist Rachel Claudio, among countless many others. So now, I will follow this gift of Poetry where ever she may lead Me,

humbled to have an audience that will listen, and a venue to perform My Craft.

I was also fortunate in My Time to also Host, the Famous, *"Panoramic Poetry"* every 2nd & 3rd Friday of the Month, downtown Philly, One of, if not the Oldest Longest Running Poetry Venues in the City of Philadelphia, sponsored by the Famous "October Gallery." As well as *"Uptown Panoramic Poetry"* every First & Last Sunday of the Month, in Philly, with My Talented Poetic Co-Hosts Allen Turner & RealEyes Mi, which too was sponsored by the "October Gallery." Then it was *"Poetic Vibez"* along with My Talented Co-Host DJ Unbreakable, and Our House Band "Best Kept Soul," & and also the Visual Art Stylings of Our House Painter Don Stephens, once every (3) months. Then last, but not least, *"Poetry & Praise-Café Zion"* every 1st Saturday of the month. A Spiritual Based Poetry Venue, where secular artists were Welcomed. We had from Poets, Singers, Praise Dancers, & Comedians all with the Live Talented "MTM Band." Just as recent as March 2020, I was a part of a Dynamic Collective, that I was hoping to Expand My Poetry, and do Great Things with here in Delaware, where I now reside, it was called *"Diverse Verses,"* but due to circumstances beyond My Control, it seems from My Opinion, Creative Differences, caused issues …

But if interested, I can be reached for conversation, and bookings at Crucialpoet@yahoo.com or of course on Facebook at www.facebook.com/PoetCrucial or My Artist Page at www.facebook.comCrucialpoet.

Artie Bryant

I began to nurture my love for poetry many years ago. I crossed that inevitable time of turbulence on my life path and I relied on the words of poetry to provide a healing to my mind, spirit and soul. At that time, I read a lot of poetry and slowly began to write more and more. I immediately fell in love with the therapeutic feeling I obtained from writing my feelings and emotions in a rhythmic stanza. Writing became a top hobby for me and was a stress reliever in this life and world of nonstop movement.

The Poet Crucial and I met many years ago on a sports chat forum. I'm a huge sports fan and I have been into sports by either playing or coaching most of my life. I grew up in a small town in Prince George's county of the state of Maryland. In the cracks and crevices of the concrete in my hometown of Bladensburg is where I learned any and everything about life. Bladensburg taught me how to always be tougher than the tough times I face. In my late 30s a friend invited me into a group chat of fellas who talked sports talk multiple times a day. While dealing with a rocky marriage that was heading to an eventual divorce, this forum of sports talk became my outlet and needed therapy. Our group chats started to veer away from solely discussing sports and started to become this incredible daily fellowship of men discussing everything from trending sports news to families and personal problems. The most unique aspect of this chat group is that majority of us had never met face to face. We fellowshipped for many years by group emails only and the inspiration/support was as if we all grew up in the same neighborhood and played on the same playgrounds since childhood. Our group consisted of about 20 guys from all spectrums of the world and we named ourselves the JLSC (Joy Luck Sports Club). Crucial and I would chat periodically off-line about poetry. I knew of his involvement and I knew that he had an interest in performing his art. For years we chatted in a jokingly way about one day writing a poetry book together, however both of our busy lives kept this thought just that. I have a purpose and gift to touch young adult's lives in a positive way through the vehicle of coaching. I coached high school basketball for 15 years in Washington DC. I am a divorced father of 3 and I am on my 32nd year of service to the federal government. To say my life stays busy is an understatement.

This incredible life that I have been afforded has come with many highs and many lows. My passion for writing has been therapy through most of my life experiences. Crucial and I decided that it's time for our thoughts of a joint poetry project of life to become a world reality. I am overly excited to share and bring to you our Selfless Letters of Caring Desires and Scorned Egos. I hope you enjoyed our project of inspirational joys and realities of life.